12 SECONDS IN THE DARK

12 SECONDS IN THE DARK

A POLICE OFFICER'S FIRSTHAND ACCOUNT
OF THE BREONNA TAYLOR RAID

SGT. JOHN MATTINGLY

12 Seconds in the Dark: A Police Officer's Firsthand Account of the Breonna Taylor Raid

ISBN: 978-1-956007-01-5

Cover design by David Fassett
Pages 40, 41, 42, and 44, photo credit: Dr. Bill Smock
Page 103, photo credit: AP

First Edition

Published by DW Books
DW Books is a division of Daily Wire

Daily Wire
1831 12th Avenue South
Suite 460
Nashville, TN 37203

www.dailywire.com

PRINTED IN THE USA

For Jenna

CONTENTS

CHAPTER 1

THE FOUNDATION

As she lay there bleeding out, we could hear the gut-wrenching screams coming from the other room that only a mother could produce.

Just minutes earlier, it had been just another day of looking for a murder suspect that our unit was tasked with. As we left the 2nd Division, a call came out over the radio. There was a shooting involving a small child. Only about a minute away, we were the first to arrive at the scene. We heard a TV on in the front room as we approached the house. With guns drawn, we banged on the door and announced our presence. There was no answer initially. In these situations, you pray it was just a prank call. As relief was setting in, we saw a small boy peeking out the window. We waved at the little guy and asked him to come open the door. I could see the fear in his wide eyes. At this point, my heart sank. My pulse was pounding in my neck as the realization hit that this was not a prank call. In this situation, as with most 911 calls, you have no idea what you are about to encounter once you enter that door. The young boy unlocked the security door. We quickly assessed the scene and started to clear the room—this is a common tactic used when searching a house/building to make sure it is safe to continue the search or rescue attempt. As we entered the kids' room, we came across the scene that every officer dreads.

Blood and brain matter were splattered on the wall, and the lifeless body of a small child lay on the floor in a puddle of blood. Donnie, a paramedic before becoming a police officer, was the first one through the door and immediately started rendering first aid and chest compressions. We flipped the mattress out of the way to assist and make room for EMS. On the floor next to the dresser was a .38 caliber revolver. The unforgettable smell of gun powder mixed with the iron smell of blood filled the room. We continued to perform chest compressions and rescue breathing on this beautiful three-year-old angel who had tragically been shot while playing with her teenage brother's handgun. EMS showed up a short time later and took the lifeless body to the hospital even though they knew she was gone. I was the one who had to tell the mother her baby girl had passed. I hugged this poor woman as she cried and collapsed in my arms.

I felt her anguish as any decent human being would. It's especially hard when you have kids yourself and can empathize. You see, life isn't fair. There's no real rhyme or reason that our finite human minds can understand when tragedies take place around us. We were raised to believe God has a plan in everything He allows, but sometimes, in these situations, I still ask WHY?

The mother explained to me that her sixteen-year-old son had given her trouble for years. She had kicked him out of the house previously due to him selling drugs and having guns. She had a five-year-old son and three-year-old daughter that she needed to protect from that lifestyle, she exclaimed. Just recently, the older son had begged to come home and promised he had turned his life around. The day before this accident, she had allowed him to return home for one last chance. That last chance cost her baby's life.

That night, the older son had gone with some friends and left a loaded .38 revolver, with the hammer back, sitting on the dresser in the kids' bedroom. The three-year-old girl saw the gun, and standing on her tiptoes, put her hand on the gun. The five-year-old brother saw this happening and attempted to stop her in an effort to protect his little sister. As he grabbed the gun in her hand, he accidentally pulled the trigger, and the unimaginable happened. Though trying to save her, this poor boy has to live the rest of his life with the guilt of his sister's death. This heartbroken mother has to live with the guilt that she wasn't able to protect her youngest because she was trying to save her oldest. There's never a win in these tragedies.

In 1991, I was eighteen years old and felt invincible. We were on our senior trip in high school, eating at a Pizza Hut somewhere in southeast Texas. I looked out the window and saw a female employee arguing with a guy I assumed was her boyfriend. The girl looked scared as the older guy was berating her. He was so infuriated that he punched her in the face.

Without hesitation, and definitely without thinking it through, I jumped to my feet and ran outside to confront the guy, or should I say, the coward. I had no training and no plan, but as I yelled and approached him, he jumped in his car and sped off. My adrenaline was pumping, but I was relieved he had decided to leave. The young girl was crying but managed to muster up a "thank you" as she sheepishly went back inside through the employees' door. The heart-pumping adrenaline rush didn't compare to the feeling of being able to help a defenseless person. It was then that I decided I wanted to be a cop.

I grew up in Louisville, Kentucky, in a poverty-stricken part of town commonly referred to as Portland. It was a very proud community, but there were hurdles to get over if you wanted to succeed. Crime was high. I saw many kids turn to running drugs for the local, well-known drug dealers. I would see them come into the local grocery store with their "Portland Fades"—that was the name of the haircut all the cool kids would get from Myers Barber Shop located in the heart of the neighborhood—while wearing their new Jordans. These same kids with the latest shoes, fresh haircuts, and rope gold chains would have to go home to their run-down houses where they were lucky to have any air or heat and often very little to no love from their abusive, alcoholic, or drug-addicted parents. It's understandable why these young kids would turn to the local drug dealers, who seemed to have everything they didn't have in life, as their means of survival. Seeing these dealers take advantage of these kids and their situations while simultaneously ruining their lives and the lives of so many in my community gave me an abhorrence for drug dealers. I despised the destruction of families I watched over the years, so it's no wonder that my desire from early on in my police career was to protect the community by getting drug dealers off the streets.

I was very fortunate. I tell people that I am from Portland, but Portland didn't raise me. My parents are very conservative Christians, and I was sheltered from many of the pitfalls that growing up in an impoverished area presented. My dad has been a Baptist preacher since before I was born, pastoring Shawnee Baptist Church in the Portland neighborhood for thirty-seven years, and at the age of seventy-seven, he is still going strong in a smaller church in Indiana.

From as far back as my memory serves, our church had a very diverse congregation. There were black, white, and Hispanic members. While we had a few congregants who were well-off, many average, paycheck-to-paycheck families, and a slew who were poverty-stricken or even desolate. We had everything from doctors to business owners to those who never finished high school. Our church had several bus routes that would go into the inner city and bring hundreds of kids to church each Sunday. The kids would get a hamburger or some type of treat before they went home. The first priority was always to present the gospel of Christ, but we also knew church provided an escape to show these kids that someone loved them and cared for them, even if for only a few hours a week.

There were a lot of sacrifices growing up in an inner-city church preacher's home. My father is the ultimate example of service and sacrifice and taught me at a young age that we do good things for others out of compassion and not for anything in return. The majority of the people that we ministered to had nothing to give back, and that was okay because it was the example that Christ taught us. These early experiences set me up for my destiny and calling as a public servant.

When I came out of the academy in 2000, I was married to my first wife—yes, I'm a police divorce statistic—and we had three kids under the age of four. I started my police career a little later than I had wanted to at age twenty-seven, but I was ready to make a difference. The excitement of going to work was like a dream come true. I would have done the job for free at this point in my career.

During the first five and a half years of my police career, I worked the graveyard shift, midnight to 8 a.m. with a six-day on and two-day off rotation. Several days a week, we would have court, which started at 9 a.m. The schedule is brutal on your body and family life. During this time early in my career, my disdain for defense attorneys (even though most are good people) was born. The attorneys knew many of the more eager police officers—the ones who locked a lot of people up—worked the late shift. They would put us in a holding pattern and try to wait us out, knowing that after a long night and several hours of sitting in a courthouse, you just wanted to go home. Many times, they won. This manipulative game is one of the many problems in our justice system as a whole, a topic I'll touch more on later.

My first sixteen weeks of training on the street were in the Portland neighborhood where I not only grew up but still lived. It was surreal working with the cops I had seen on a daily basis at the convenience stores or McDonald's—and, in turn, locking up some people I had played basketball with at the community parks. Every trip to the local food market was an adventure to find out who I would lock up this week, and who wanted to kick my butt when they saw me in public. Fortunately, I treated people the way I would want my mom and dad or my kids treated because there had been times I had been stopped by police—driving late at night in the high-crime area where I lived—and it wasn't always a pleasant experience. I was talked down to and at times accused of things I didn't do, so I vowed that I would NOT treat people with disrespect even before I became a police officer.

The first years are always the most exciting. It was like living the "best of" *COPS* episodes several times a week. My very first run on my first day on the streets with my Field Training Officer involved an eighty-something-year-old deceased female. When we walked into her room, it was apparent she had fallen out of her bed and passed away on the cold wood floor all alone. She had a thin nightgown on and no underclothes. This wasn't the first dead body I had seen, but it was the first one that I had to check the pulse on. I confirmed she was gone, even though she had obviously been deceased for a while. Seeing a dead body and actually touching a dead person are two different and unnerving experiences.

During the next shift, I made my first homicide run. We were dispatched to a shooting in the Clarksdale housing projects. As we climbed the stairs to the second-floor apartment, I was presented with my first smell of the gun powder/blood mix I mentioned earlier. It was also my first experience with the death gurgle, which is when a person is dead or close to it, and their body is still trying to breathe. You can hear the blood gurgling in their throat as their body sometimes twitches with reflexes. This individual had been shot in the side of the head while sitting in his recliner. His skull and brain matter were embedded in the wall next to him, and his eyes were wide open. I tried to act like I had been there and done that, but I'm sure I looked like a deer in headlights.

Any time we made a significant run in the projects, people would amass in large groups to see what had happened and check on their family and friends, and this was no exception. While the projects were full of what most of society would think are dysfunctional people, they were a community all to their own with their own set of internal rules and repercussions for breaking those rules. As I learned, one of the main rules was, do not talk to the police; more importantly, if you do speak to the police, do not be a rat. Most of the time, when we asked, no one heard or saw anything, but in this case, someone said the individual committed suicide. There was one problem: no weapon. The .45 caliber handgun used to kill this victim was found in a trash can about 300 feet from the building. It's kind of hard to shoot yourself in the head and throw the gun away outside of your residence. This was my first experience with the tension between police and the community we were there to protect and serve. I was sincerely there to help this community and the family of this victim, so I was dumbfounded that this was the code within the community and felt sad that it hindered the help we could provide. The learning curve is quick on the streets, and if you don't keep up with the curve, you fail miserably. Failing can lead to lawsuits, to being fired, indictments, injuries, or even worse—death.

The excitement didn't stop after my training phases; as a matter of fact, it was just getting started. I was placed on a late-watch crew that was very proactive. I don't want to offend any of my other bosses in the police department because I have had many, but my first lieutenant (Joe Manning) and sergeant (Chuck Tilford) were the best command duo I ever worked for. They were the perfect balance for each other and the many new officers in the late watch. Lt. Manning was the enforcer who had you shaking in your boots if you were called into his office, while Sgt. Tilford was the loving father figure who had the amazing ability to put you at ease.

Sgt. Tilford was a chain smoker who actually had stopped smoking for quite some time, that is until our crew wreaked havoc on him (in a good way) with our aggressive work ethic and practical jokes. At one point, we covered the walls in his office with hats and artifacts we had collected over time. Another time, one of the officers thought it would be funny to place a used toilet that had been left on the sidewalk for trash pickup in his office. Our district major didn't find it so amusing the next morning and ordered that we clear anything not related to police matters out of the office by the end of our next shift. What a stick in the mud! Needless to say, Sgt. Tilford began smoking again shortly after our crew was assembled. My sincerest apologies, Mrs. Tilford.

In my third year in the department, I was assigned the same beat on late watch as Mike Campbell, a heck of a cop who had been my last training officer at the academy and became a good friend. Mike would later be one of the groomsmen in my second wedding and, interestingly, was with me the night I was shot on March 13, 2020. This particular night we received the call of a lady screaming in an apartment. As we approached the door, we could hear someone inside screaming for help. I kicked open the front door, expecting it to be a domestic dispute. Unfortunately, domestic abuse is an all-too-common call, but to my surprise, what we encountered was a forcible stranger rape in progress. Usually, police are reactive in cases such as this—you either take a report or call sex crimes, and they take control of the scene. This situation was different. The suspect jumped out of a window and fled on foot. I was much younger and in better shape then, and the chase was on. Fortunately, I caught the suspect, and the on-call sex crimes detective responded. The suspect was found guilty in court. Situations like this are why I wanted to do this job. For that small moment in time, I made a difference in someone's life. I couldn't undo the damage that was inflicted on this poor woman, but I was able to help bring her some justice and peace of mind knowing this animal would not attack her again.

I remember when methamphetamine labs blew up, some literally! The first search warrant I served on an active meth lab was sometime in 2003 or 2004. I was still on late-watch patrol and stopped a truck leaving a local pool hall that was a constant problem location. The occupant of the truck had an array of drugs and guns in the car. This guy fit the typical drug-dealer stereotype that television and movies depict. He was a tall, thin, white male with long, greasy, dark hair and a beard. He had tattoos—which weren't as mainstream as they are now—and rode motorcycles. This arrest led to a search of his house.

I contacted a friend, Tony James, who was in our division's FLEX unit, and he gladly came out to the scene and helped me draft the warrant, gather a team of guys, and execute the warrant. Tony had graduated from the academy with me and had the same desire to work narcotics as I did. Tony was also present with me the night I was shot and was the one who helped save my life with the tourniquet he was carrying in his vest. (Do you see a pattern here?) As soon as we went through the door to clear the house, we could smell the noxious odors that burned our throats and eyes. Meth labs were fairly new in this region, and there weren't many protocols at the time to protect officers and citizens when dealing with these labs. This was my first, but far from my last, dealing with methamphetamines.

Meth users, and more specifically cooks, are a peculiar breed. They are collectors of knives and glass pipes ("chicken bones"). They love to take electronics apart and try to fix them, and every single one has an array of sex toys and pornography. It's a whole different world than the average law-abiding citizen will ever encounter. I remember about two hours into searching this house, my entire face from my chin to above my nose was numb from all the chemicals in the air from the large, active glass beakers full of cooking meth. We didn't yet understand the volatility of these labs nor the dangerous and deadly effects of these chemicals on one's lungs. I've had asthma since I was nine years old, and I don't think it's ever been the same since this warrant.

We had a point of contact in our narcotics unit that responded to the scene. He collected samples from each of the beakers for court purposes and poured the rest down the sewer drain outside the house. This all seems insane looking back. It was maybe a year later that stringent national protocols were put in place for meth labs. They were now deemed hazardous scenes, as they should be, and if you were exposed in any way, the boys from the fire department received great pleasure in stripping you down and hosing you off in the middle of the street. It didn't matter if it was 100 degrees or 0 degrees out. If you got exposed . . . you got hosed.

In 2005, I interviewed and won a spot in the 4th Division's FLEX unit. The 4th Division had it all. We had homes that were historic and worth over a million dollars, two low-income housing projects, and areas that were middle class. Still, the majority was low income and full of impoverished citizens. Crack was still the drug of choice, and there was an abundance of crack houses. The FLEX unit was a plainclothes, division-based unit that served the needs of the individual divisions throughout the department. We were used for theft, robbery, and prostitution details, but the main purpose was to attack the drug issues. We were basically small six-to-eight-man drug units that were very proactive—jumping street corners and conducting investigations that usually ended with search warrants. Drugs were the driving factor in most of the issues that we were facing. We've all seen how drugs destroy families and communities.

After five and a half years on patrol, this was just the jolt I needed to rejuvenate my spirit and rekindle my love of police work. I learned new skills and saw a whole new side of people's private lives that I never really wanted to view. You see, when you conduct search warrants, you go through everything . . . I mean everything! This will come into play later on in this book when discussing the search warrant at Breonna Taylor's apartment.

After a couple of years in FLEX, the drug scene started to shift. Crack was still a drug of choice for some, but the opioid scene came on with a vengeance. We started seeing young people from every socioeconomic background affected by this epidemic. Sure, drugs have always been in every end of town and not limited by race or gender, but this was different. This was a game-changer. The pills were everywhere and easy to get. Doctors were prescribing them like candy, and there was no shortage of a sweet tooth for this devil. Weed was still a staple, but kids now had pill parties. It was turning them into zombies who couldn't get enough to feed their addictions.

I remember an investigation that led us to an apartment in the south end of Louisville. The target of this investigation was a Middle Eastern male who was selling OxyContin by the hundreds. After we made entry and cleared the apartment, we began looking around to ensure it was safe to begin our search. Hanging on the wall was a large picture of the Twin Towers and the surrounding area. I could feel my blood pressure rising. Another detective on the scene reached out to the FBI with this guy's information. He was not only on the no-fly list, but he was on the terrorist watch list with ties to terrorist organizations. It was determined that he was sending money from the drug proceeds back to fund the fight against America. We found almost 10,000 OxyContin pills, cash, and a weapon in his apartment. The Feds took custody of him, and he was deported out of the country. A couple of years ago, I received a call that the same suspect had been arrested again in the United States. Drugs are not only destroying us from within, but the proceeds are being used to attack us from the outside as well. It's time to wake up and stop painting the police, who risk their lives to combat this epidemic, as the bad guys.

I had a great FLEX career. We served no less than five search warrants per week, and I was always fortunate to have great partners who were capable and trustworthy. We had our share of car chases, fights, and some scary times, but it was where I felt at home.

In 2009, my sergeant at the time, Mindy Baker, encouraged me to take the sergeant's test. I originally said, "NO WAY!" I had no desire to climb the ranks of the police department. I was doing what I loved and wanted to get into the narcotics division. However, at the time, I started to see the passing of the guard. The older generation was starting to retire, and people who had come on after me were being promoted. I also had been on long enough to realize that not everyone in a leadership position was a true leader. Some were totally incompetent at their jobs. Mindy looked at me and said, "You can either work *for* them or work *with* them." Enough said and point taken.

The sergeant's exam was only three weeks away, and the study material was a mountain of papers. You had to study the Kentucky law book, the Fraternal Order of Police (FOP) contract, and a never-ending SOP (Standard Order of Procedure). While I'm not a savant, I'm also not an idiot, but I must admit I do not like reading. I crammed in everything I could and ended up tying five people for thirty-third on the written test. So essentially, I was number thirty-seven. That's not too great since only about nine spots would be open at the time of promotions. While I didn't have the same amount of time as the others to study for the written test, I was on an even playing field for the oral assessment, which played a large role in the promotion process. I studied like my career depended on it because, as much as I like winning, I hate to lose or be embarrassed by a bad performance. I worked hard and, fortunately, jumped significantly. I remember being on my way home from work when my sergeant called me. She said, "Jon, have you seen the list?" I told her I hadn't. She went on to tell me I was number five. I had jumped thirty-two people. I thought she was messing with me, but thankfully she wasn't. I was pumped. When I look back

on the four guys who finished ahead of me, three ended up majors, and the other is a current lieutenant colonel on the department and a friend.

I never studied for another promotional test. I took one out of curiosity but didn't put any time into it. The phrase is that you only become a sergeant to be a lieutenant because s*#t flows up to sergeants from officers and down from lieutenants.

I've been blessed and have had an amazing career that is the stuff movies are made of. I've seen things that the average citizen wouldn't believe. I've always had incredible, go-getter officers working for me. Plus, I wasn't naive to the politics in the department. I've seen some guys get promoted to lieutenant, and they change. They become politicians or backstabbers—those two are really one and the same—to get to the next level. I had no desire to be that guy simply for power or prestige. Heck, they forget your name two months after you retire anyway, so why go against all my morals and destroy friendships and my reputation for a place that replaces you with the next person up? No thanks!

I've been told I'm crazy for staying a sergeant, but I always loved the job I was in when the tests came around. I loved the fact that a sergeant can be a leader, a buffer from the administration, and still do actual police work. I was home.

CHAPTER 2

LEARNING HOW TO LEAD FROM THE FRONT

It was different being the boss and not one of the guys, but the next ten years were full of more excellent police work, as well as some frustrating run-ins with ineffective leaders. Nonetheless, I had some great team members and made some lifelong friends, several of whom would be with me the fateful night of March 13, 2020.

It was 2010 when we encountered a scenario that was remarkably similar to the night Breonna Taylor lost her life. I still had the narcotics bug in me even though I was back on patrol. One of the guys who had come to my platoon—Mike Halbleib, known as Hobble Wobble on the streets—was a legend in our narcotics unit when I was a young officer. He was a master at cultivating informants. He would have guys he hadn't talked to in years call him out of the blue and give him great information just because they liked the guy. Mike still had some juice left in him after over twenty years on the job and wanted to teach some of the younger guys how to conduct narcotics investigations properly.

After a long investigation into a group of drug dealers that were moving multiple kilos of cocaine inside car haulers from Tennessee to Louisville, Mike was ready to execute a warrant on one of the players. On this particular night, a prosecutor with the Commonwealth Attorney's Office was coming along for the ride since he would be the main prosecutor on the case. We briefed the warrant with the assistance of the division's FLEX unit. After formulating a plan, we made our approach on the house.

We had several officers assisting on this warrant, and I was designated as the cover officer at the point of entry. The side door was determined to be the best point of entry. There was a glass storm door over a metal door that had glass halfway down the front. Several times in the past, I'd found that this type of glass storm door would pop open with a quick hard pull even if it was locked. I checked the door, and naturally, it was locked. We knocked on the door and began to announce, "Police! Search warrant!" After several knocks, I moved up to open the storm door for the breaching officer so he could ram the door open. I gave the door a hard yank, but it didn't open. Instead, the door handle broke in half, and I was left holding it in my hand. I threw the handle on the ground and stepped back to cover the door with my pistol so they could ram the door.

As soon as I stepped back, a gunshot went off from inside the house. Everything slowed down to almost a halt. It was like a scene in *The Matrix*. The glass from the storm door was coming at me in what appeared to be a whirlwind, the pieces of the glass moving through the air in slow motion. The bullet whizzed within inches of my head and through the privacy fence behind me. The glass from the door cut my forearms where I had my arms extended with my weapon. The door had large faux wood blinds on it, so the bullet just ripped through them and gave my ear a high five as it went past my skull. I didn't return fire because I couldn't see who had fired through the door.

We retreated for cover and called the suspect out of the house. After a few minutes he emerged from the house with his hands in the air. My adrenaline was still up when we took him into custody. I can still recall the sound of the glass from the shattered storm door crackling under my feet as we escorted him back in the house. I remember the look of disbelief and shock on the prosecutor's face. While he had prosecuted many suspects in court, this was his first experience seeing the process cops go through before a case landed on his desk.

The suspect was arrested that night and served almost seven years for shooting at the police. He used the same defense that many others have used, including Breonna's boyfriend, Kenneth Walker. This suspect claimed, just like Walker, that he didn't know we were the police, and he was scared. Since this was years before body cameras, the lack of footage didn't automatically make the officers liars and the criminals the best witnesses ever, thankfully. Having the Commonwealth Attorney on the scene and almost a victim was the next best thing to footage and helped put all those BS claims to bed. In this case, unlike Walker, the suspect realized he messed up and surrendered in a timely manner. Had Kenny done that, Breonna might be alive today.

The parallels don't end there. Had I returned fire, I could have killed two innocent people that night. Through that side door we were banging on was a kitchen. On the back wall of that kitchen was an adjoining wall to the master bedroom where the suspect's girlfriend and a newborn were lying in bed. That wall and their bed would have been in the direct line of fire had we been forced to shoot. I'm blessed I was not hit that night, and I'm thankful no innocent person was hurt. Head shots are a lot less forgiving than leg shots, and had I been hit, I can't say for certain that shots would not have been returned and another innocent life tragically lost.

After a year on late watch, I was offered the opportunity to go to the district detective office, and I worked there for about a year and a half. It was a different pace for me. It involved a lot of paperwork, a shirt and tie, and many, many meetings about the same stuff over and over. It was like *Groundhog Day*, and it's just not my thing. I really enjoyed the people I worked with, and I learned a lot. I just did not enjoy the work itself. Besides, I had my eye on the FLEX unit sergeant spot, as I knew that guy was coming up on retirement.

In mid-2012, I transferred to the FLEX position in the 8th Division. It was a slower paced FLEX than others in the city because the division encompassed a demographic with higher incomes. There weren't people hanging out on street corners. We didn't have the calls for service or the complaints on drug dealers and houses like we did in the 4th Division, but there was still plenty of dope to be seized. I had worked in the urban part of the city for ten years before coming to the land of milk and honey, and you know what happened? I got shot at (again) while serving a warrant. There is crime in every part of every city.

It was in this unit that I had a young detective working for me named Myles Cosgrove. Call it coincidence if you'd like, but I call it fate. I built a relationship with Myles in 2012. In 2020, eight years later, Myles would be standing over top of me and protecting me after I had been shot. This was God laying the groundwork years in advance for a life-altering situation for both of us in the future.

In that FLEX unit, I was finally back home doing what I enjoyed doing, but this didn't last long. After all these years, I was actually getting to do two things in life I enjoyed: dope work and still having a little time to sit down with a nice cup of coffee once in a while. This was all about to change. Louisville's homicide and violent crime spiked in 2012, putting the city into a frenzy. The city council, the media, and the citizens were all asking what could be done. A new unit, the VIPER unit, was formed to combat the worst of the worst criminals.

It was mid-September 2012, and I got the call from Lt. Kit Steimle one afternoon. "Johnny, whatcha doin'?" Crap. I knew exactly what he wanted. I liked Kit, but I had no desire to work for this guy. He was brilliant but a little too cocky for me. Knowing my lack of tolerance for cocky leaders, I was afraid that it wouldn't be a good fit, and I'd be miserable. He made his pitch, and I politely told him I appreciated the offer but was content where I was. He said a few choice curse words of encouragement and hung up on me.

I worked an off-duty job with Mike Nobles that summer, and we became friendly. He's a heck of a storyteller, so he kept me entertained. Mike was the ram guy the night of the Breonna Taylor warrant and held my hand on scene when my lieutenant tightened the tourniquet so hard I thought I saw Jesus. He's the fourth guy from my past who was on the scene and helped save my life the night I was shot. God sure knows what He's doing. He put a handful of guys in my life way before the Breonna Taylor tragedy that He knew I would need to be a crucial part of those events.

Anyway, Mike has a persuasive way about him, and he begged me to be his sergeant in this new VIPER unit that was forming. Mike and Lt. Steimle were already good friends, so Mike knew he had a job waiting. Needless to say, over the course of a couple of weeks, I agreed to the job and have zero regret for taking it. I worked harder, had more fun, and learned more in the next three years than I had the previous twelve.

The VIPER Unit began operations in October of 2012. The unit was comprised of highly driven alpha males who wanted to be in the middle of the most dangerous part of the city and deal with the most hardened, violent gang members and criminals. It wasn't unusual on any given day, usually several times a week, to find yourself in the middle of a vehicle- or foot-pursuit with a suspect wanted for murder, assault, robbery, or another violent crime. That's what we were tasked to do, and we were good at that job.

I thought I had worked hard during my time on the police force, but I was in for a rude awakening. Our days consisted of fast-paced work that

had a specific agenda. Many nights we worked through dinner or stopped late at night and ate Taco Bell in our vehicles. We were on ten-hour shifts, and many nights we worked eleven or twelve hours. Those extra hours were donated because the overtime was not in the budget. We went home every night exhausted but returned to work the next day excited to be there and ready to go. I attribute some of that to Lt. Steimle. I was afraid he would be a micromanager and a know-it-all, but he turned out to be the opposite. He trusted us to do our jobs and did his best to make work a fun environment. One of the perks of the job was when there was an event downtown and I could go meet the family for a few and take the opportunity to see them.

In police work, it's important not to have the reins too tight on people. Chuck Tilford, my first sergeant I mentioned earlier, gave me this advice when, after I was promoted, I asked, if there was only one thing he could tell me, what it would be. His answer was simple but often overlooked: *The city has entrusted these individuals with a gun and badge and the ability to take away someone's freedom, so treat them like adults and let them do their jobs.* That advice has stuck with me throughout my career as a supervisor, and when new officers come to work for me that came from a micro-managing boss, I see them light up and become so much better at what they do because they are trusted and allowed to do their jobs.

Our lieutenant colonel at that time, Yvette Gentry, was a tough but fair boss. She led by example and always had our back, as long as we were doing the right thing. The two previous years before starting the VIPER unit, our city had seen record numbers of homicides and assaults, and Col.

Gentry understood the dynamics of the neighborhoods we were tasked to protect. She had a connection with the community from years of community meetings, outreach programs, and service herself in those same areas. Col. Gentry, a female person of color, was known in the community as tough on crime but also fair, compassionate, and willing to listen. These attributes made her the perfect fit for the challenges that lay ahead.

During this time, you could see and feel the rise of a younger, bolder generation of kids carrying guns. Their respect toward anyone in authority was dwindling. The old Gs, some of whom were hardened criminals, would say these "young cats" were scary and out of control. There were no more fistfights or settling beefs. It was all about shoot first and worry about consequences later. The code on the streets was changing as well. The hierarchy within the gangs was no longer a thing. Kids were just out doing whatever they wanted to whomever they wanted with no older members holding them accountable. Car-jackings, homicides, assaults, and total chaos abounded. As a unit, VIPER was given a longer leash. It was almost like policing when I first became an officer: nothing illegal and no violating civil rights, just no-nonsense, hands-on policing. It wasn't long until word was on the street that the "jump out boys"—that's what they named us—meant business. There wasn't a day that went by that we weren't in precarious situations and getting illegal guns off of violent people. Over the next three years, the City of Louisville saw significant decreases in the homicide rate. I would like to think our aggressive unit helped make the difference.

Col. Gentry retired in 2015, and new leadership came in wanting to put their own spin on things that were already working. We went from a kick-butt productive unit getting over 600 guns off the streets a year to a unit told what side of the street we had to stay on because they had agreed to that with the community. How crazy is it that the "woke" citizens groups, not crime data, decide where a specialty unit can police to reduce and deter crime? We were told when to eat lunch, regardless of whether we were hungry or not. We were also told we could no longer execute search warrants on suspects with drugs and guns if they weren't already violent convicted felons—even though we had been able to convict many assault and murder suspects over the course of the previous three years by search warrants that didn't fit that criterion.

The senior homicide sergeant at the time had fawned over our unit, saying we were making Homicide look like rock stars. Through our informants, we had been getting homicide leads on cases where they had none, locating and arresting their suspects, and doing all this within days of the crimes being committed. So, needless to say, we were all flabbergasted when the new rules were implemented, and it didn't take long before the disgruntlement set in.

Shortly after these new guidelines were put in place, we got word of a violent felon with drugs and guns in a house just outside of these new "target areas" that the new bosses had implemented without any consultation from the guys who had been pounding the streets for the past three years with great success. When I asked to do the warrant, I was denied. Being the driven leader that I am and wanting to actually make a difference and not just a rank, we executed the warrant the following day after persuading a different commander of the necessity.

As we entered the house, the suspect and I made eye contact. He had a gun in his hand, but it wasn't in a threatening position. He threw the gun in a trash can in the kitchen and tried to escape. We caught him and recovered the weapon along with a load of heroin and cocaine. He was a persistent felony offender, but better yet, the gun he threw in the trash turned out to have been used in a homicide a week earlier.

As we came into the office with our bounty of seized goodies, we were feeling pretty good about ourselves. The major then told us he didn't care what we'd got and said that wasn't our job anymore since we went outside the new imaginary lines. We exchanged a few words, and I went to my desk and typed up my transfer paperwork. This was the third incident where we did the job that the community needed and had asked us to do and were chastised for it. One of the incidents almost cost my detectives their lives because of the ego and incompetence of this boss. I finished my transfer request and placed it on my major's desk at midnight.

I received a call at 8:30 a.m. the next morning telling me my transfer was accepted and effective that coming weekend. I was relieved but sad at the same time. All the work we had built up was torn down in a matter of two months by ineffective leaders who refused to listen to their subordinates. It's always amazing to watch someone climb the ranks and seemingly forget how to successfully police along the way.

Within a month, almost everyone from the original VIPER unit had moved on. The unit had changed its mission statement and name to 9th Mobile. It was filled with a corps of young guys with a lot of talent and ambition but who lacked experience. Over the next few years, the homicide rate began to crawl back to previous numbers and beyond. In 2020, Louisville hit a record high of 173 homicides—160 by the use of a firearm—and had an additional 585 shooting victims who survived. That's 745 gunshot victims in a city of 750,000 citizens.

I was back on late watch, but only for a short period before receiving a call to come back to the 4th Division as the FLEX sergeant. I was excited, but it wouldn't come without some bumps in the road. My lieutenant at the time, Kim Burbrink, fought for me to get the spot. Her boss, the LTC who replaced Gentry, however, wasn't too keen on the idea since I had just recently left her unit. There were a few run-ins with the LTC and the major of the Mobile 9th during my tenure as the 4th Division FLEX sergeant, but I somehow managed to make it unscathed through that tumultuous period, thanks in part to Kim Burbrink. I'll be forever grateful to her for sticking her neck out and doing the right thing.

In October of 2016, the police department decided, in its ultimate wisdom (insert sarcasm), to eliminate all the Division FLEX units and go to a more beefed-up, county-wide narcotics unit. This was yet another attempt to put a patch on a sinking ship. The leaders at the top were scrambling to find answers to the increase in drug and violent crime-related offenses. They might have realized that reinventing the wheel doesn't always work, but no. Egos refused to admit that they made mistakes or that their new strategies weren't panning out. They could have asked the guys who were in the areas and risking their lives daily if they had any input, but no. Instead, there were constant knee-jerk reactions and changes to policy in response to any event during the tenure of the now-discredited police chief, Steve Conrad. More on that later.

In November 2016, I interviewed for and was awarded a sergeant's position in the narcotics unit. I was excited to finally make it to narcotics after sixteen years, and I was able to hand-pick the guys working for me. We had a rock star crew. I loved them, and they loved me in return and worked their butts off. Once again, I was part of a crew that worked nonstop. They loved investigations and search warrants. Many nights, our shift was scheduled to end at midnight, and I'd have to send that text to my wife saying, I'm not sure what time I'll get home. It wasn't long before we were filling tables with guns and drugs we had seized.

In mid-2017, our unit worked a case with another good friend of mine, Daryl Hyche. Daryl was a detective in VIPER who had made his way to narcotics a year before I did. (Daryl was shot in the head while in the line of duty a year later and miraculously survived.) We had already worked our ten-hour shift during this investigation, and some of the guys had gone home because of other responsibilities. It was midnight, and Brad Beckham, who worked for me and was also a great friend, approached me saying they had a tip on a possible large amount of heroin. My ears perked up, and away we went. We sat outside this particular apartment all night waiting for one of the suspects to come home.

It was around 8 a.m. when Brad got on the radio and said the suspect's car was pulling up. We approached the suspect and executed the warrant on the apartment. Inside we located seventeen pounds of heroin in a backpack in a closet in the kids' room. This warrant led us to another apartment where we located an additional twenty-five pounds of heroin (forty-two total) and somewhere around $100,000 in cash and firearms. Over $3 million in narcotics was by far the largest drug bust I had been a part of during my career.

Later that year, I transferred to our Major Case Unit where I had seven detectives assigned to me in our office and another four assigned to our federal partners at the FBI and DEA. I continued to learn while in this position. The Feds' ability to work big cases is pretty impressive. I could give you story after story from my time in this unit, but that's not what this book is about.

In the fall of 2019, I realized I only wanted to work for another four or five years in the department. Our parcel interdiction unit in narcotics was a position that would be available come September, and I thought it would be a good fit. It's a job I was offered in 2016, but at that time, I still wanted to go through doors on search warrants and do stakeouts. After talking it over with my wife, I decided I should start ramping things down. Most of the jobs I had during my career were fast-paced and adrenaline-filled, so with the finish line in sight, I needed to adjust to a more normal job, one that was less risky, or so I thought.

This unit was great. It was a small, four-man unit that seized an unbelievable amount of narcotics from the different parcel carriers. Each week, I was taken aback by the amount and ways these drugs were shipped.

It was while I was working in this unit that a manpower request for the night of March 12, 2020, was issued. I volunteered to assist on this night, which led up to the fateful early morning hours of Friday, March 13.

CHAPTER 3

HOW DID WE END UP HERE?

It was Friday, January 17, 2020, when Det. Jaynes stopped me in the narcotics office and asked if I could reach out to postal (USPS) and see if there were any packages going to Jamarcus Glover at 3003 Springfield Drive #4. I explained to Det. Jaynes that I did not have any direct contacts and LMPD did not have a relationship with postal.

A couple years prior to me joining the parcel taskforce, LMPD and the USPS leadership in Louisville had a disagreement on how things were going as a partnership. Let's just say feelings were hurt and fences were never mended. These types of immature practices in leadership always cost the people not involved more than those who had the original problem. A smaller department that operates inside our county, Shively PD, had partnered up with USPS once LMPD parted ways with them, and I had built a friendship with the sergeant and one of the detectives in that department's narcotics unit. So, when Det. Jaynes asked me to inquire about the address, I reached out to them. I sent a text with the address and name. I received a text in return stating that the name sounded familiar and that they might have intercepted a parcel with that name. I was told they would check and get back to me.

I told Det. Jaynes the information I received and that they would verify if indeed it was their target or address.

The following week I ran into the detective from the other agency while working one of the other parcel services in Louisville. I asked him if he had an update on the information that I sent him. He stated that he had talked to one of the other detectives working with Jaynes and had discovered it was in fact an individual with the last name Glover, but not Jamarcus Glover. The following day I saw Det. Jaynes in the office

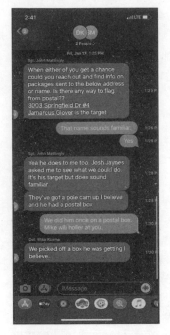

and told him of the new information. His response was, "Yeah, Kelly told me she talked to Mike and it was a different person. Shoot, I was hoping to do a rip/reversal [package delivery with immediate arrest] on the package. Now I have to do all these warrants." I told him I was sorry, and we went about our own business. That was the entire extent of my involvement before the warrants were served almost two months later.

This conversation has been a point of contention in this case since the warrant stated that the USPS postal inspector confirmed no suspicious packages being delivered to this address. I do not know to the extent of the investigation into parcels going to that address, but I do, however, know from experience that most illegal packages are not sent in the intended receiver's name. For instance, if I wanted something illegal sent to me, I would have the package sent to a fictitious name and to an address that didn't belong to me. This gives the receiver of the parcel plausible deniability, and if a search query for a suspect's name is run for parcels, it's not red-flagged because it's not in their name. So, for a postal inspector to say there were no *suspicious* packages sent to that address is a very subjective stance for him to take, especially given the negative history between this individual and LMPD.

Over the next couple of months, colonels from the chief's office would come to our office for a bi-weekly meeting with the Place-Based Investigations (PBI) Squad to talk strategy and receive updates on the unit's activity. I was consumed with my own unit, so I never attended nor was asked to attend any of these meetings. I would see the assistant chiefs in the office every other week and give the occasional nod or short conversation. Later, it was discovered that these meetings were directed at the Elliott Avenue locations—the area where Jamarcus Glover lived. Allegations have swirled that the mayor had pinpointed this location for gentrification purposes. I don't know this to be true, but after going through this painful experience of political assault on myself and those involved in this tragedy, nothing seems out of the realm of possibility. Mayor Fischer deflects any allegations directed toward him but is quick to point the finger at the police. I'll delve deeper into this topic later.

On March 9, 2020, the sergeant in charge of the Place-Based Investigations Squad sent out an email asking for assistance for a manpower intensive detail. This detail included five warrants, three to be served in the 2400 block of Elliott Ave., the fourth at 2605 Muhammed Ali, and the fifth at 3003 Springfield Dr. #4. I responded to the email by requesting for myself and Det. Nobles to be assigned to the Springfield address. I have served a couple thousand search warrants throughout my career and have been in some of the nastiest environments imaginable. I was hoping that, by choosing the residence that wasn't in a rundown part of town, I was minimizing my risk of digging through too many unseemly items. I have also participated in warrants long enough to realize that the main players would most likely be at the distribution locations, and I was hoping for less of an encounter on Springfield. I was sadly disappointed.

March 12, 2020, was a Thursday. The day had begun like any other. I conducted my daily responsibilities as well as parcel interdiction at one of the national carriers prior to the scheduled 10 p.m. briefs for the warrants, which were to take place in two separate locations. One of the lead investigators for Place-Based Investigations would brief SWAT at their office, while the detectives for the Criminal Interdiction Unit would be briefed by a supporting detective in PBI at our office.

Local attorney Sam Aguiar wants people to believe we were out drinking prior to the warrant. This is yet another false statement he added to the amended lawsuit that has zero merit. The parcel hub we go to has a sign-in sheet that we fill out, cameras everywhere, and personnel we are required to check in with. Aguiar is also the same attorney who stated, "Everyone who was part of the dirty warrant, the attempted ROBBERY of Breonna Taylor's home, her murder and the cover-up should be under internal investigation."[1]

At 9:30 I told the guys working with me at the parcel hub that we needed to leave the facility and return to the office for the briefs. I stopped by a gas station on the way to the office and got a Diet Coke from the fountain

---

[1]   Sam Aguiar Facebook post, September 21, 2020, https://www.facebook.com/sam. aguiar.986/posts/10102553716393699

machine. By the time I got to the office, the parking lot was starting to fill up with detectives for the warrants. The bright, full moon was out, and I parked my car and went inside the office. It was a room full of approximately forty-five detectives, along with Lt. Colonel LaVita Chavous. I took my place somewhere in the middle of the briefing room. I took a picture of the whiteboard on my phone so I could have the plan readily available to look back on. I'm thankful I did. Later that picture was used to show that the warrant had been changed to a "knock and announce" warrant unlike the narrative that the attorneys and media have pushed.

The brief went like most briefs do. There were a few changes to where personnel were allocated, but for the most part, things went as planned. We were told that the warrants were all signed as no-knocks, but since they had trackers and phone pings on the main targets, the no-knock would *not* be utilized at the Springfield location. We were told that there was a possibility that drugs, money, and documents connecting Glover to Taylor would be at this location. Jamarcus Glover and Breonna Taylor had dated off and on for a while. The investigators had photos and videos of Glover coming and going from Taylor's residence. There were also videos of Taylor in the car with Glover pulling up to the location on Elliot. The intel we were given was that they expected it to be only Breonna Taylor at the apartment. They were unsure about children or animals. We were asked to give Taylor *more time than normal* to answer the door. While this request was unusual, it wasn't unrealistic. I was obliged to give extended time and make this process as simple as possible with little drama. Unfortunately, that didn't work out.

After the brief I went to the closet that housed some of the entry tools and retrieved a ram and pick in case no one answered the door. Here's where things started to go downhill. I went outside with the tools in my hand. At this point it had begun to rain. When I approached my car to put the tools in, I realized I had two flat tires on both driver's side wheels. The car directly behind mine had a flat tire as well. I'm not sure if this was a coincidence or malicious. I was frustrated but didn't have time to dwell on it since my crew had a pre-planned location to meet up for the warrant and they were already en route. I ran back into the office and retrieved some keys for one of our pool cars. By the time I located the car and began to transfer my equipment, the skies had opened up and I was soaked. I moved as fast as I could to get all the equipment I needed and arrive at the rally point in time.

As I turned into the meet location, I saw Louisville Metro EMS sitting in the parking lot. I pulled up next to the ambulance to touch base and verify that they were there for us. The driver of the ambulance had some large headphones on and didn't notice me next to him, and the passenger was watching something on his phone. I don't blame them for taking some down time as they have a tough job, are short-staffed, and regularly run double shifts. I used my flashlight to get the driver's attention. He rolled his window down and attempted to take his headphones off, which got caught in his hair. Both of these EMS workers were young enough to be my kids. I asked if they were here for the warrants on Springfield. They responded, yes, and I told them it would be a little after midnight before we approached the house. They acknowledged the plan and pulled to a different spot in the parking lot. I remember thinking to myself, *I hope these guys don't have to save my life*. It was nothing personal. They just seemed unengaged.

By this time the rain had stopped. I remember looking at my phone to see it was 11:11 p.m. I texted my wife, "1111 make a wish." She responded that the text made her smile. We exchanged a few more texts, and it ended with her telling me she was going to sleep and saying, "please please be careful. I want you coming home to me." It was just after midnight at this point, making it Friday the 13th with a full moon. What could go wrong? Well, along with two flat tires, getting soaked in the rain, and having two young EMS guys, that didn't make me all that confident.

I called the detective who had an eye on the apartment and told him I was going to do a drive-by so that I knew exactly which apartment it was to make sure we went to the right door. I stayed on the phone with the detective so he could verify the correct building and door. As I drove through the parking lot, I saw a plumbing van parked in a spot right in front of the breezeway that led us to the entry door. This would be my marker for approach to the building. The breezeway had eight apartments with entry doors: four downstairs (1–4) and four upstairs (5–8). The apartment was on the bottom floor and marked with the number "4." Facing the front of the building, it was the bottom door on the right.

Once I had my bearings on the apartments, I went back to the meeting spot. We all met in the parking lot and lined our cars up for approach to the apartments. It was about twenty minutes later that SWAT announced it was approaching Elliott Ave. because the main target was approaching the trap house (a residence where drugs are sold). We began our quarter-mile approach to the apartments. As we made the turn in our approach, SWAT was making their approach on Elliott simultaneously. The next few minutes would change the lives of those involved forever.

CHAPTER 4

KEY TO THE CITY

As we pulled into the apartment complex and made the winding curve, I was the lead car and noticed an early 2000s Toyota Sequoia sitting in front of the apartment building we were approaching. This vehicle was not in a parking spot and was perpendicular to the parked cars, so I knew the person wasn't planning on staying. My concern was who was in that car: did they go to our target apartment? and how did the detective watching the apartment miss it? I was frustrated, but knew we were already committed, so I needed to stay composed and focused. I parked my car behind the Sequoia. I exited my vehicle and checked the Sequoia to make sure there was no one inside it before continuing up to the door. I remember seeing trash in the car and a pink car seat in the back. I continued to apartment #4 with the others falling in behind me: Lt. Shawn Hoover, Det. Brett Hankison, Det. Mike Nobles, Det. Tony James, Det. Mike Campbell, and Det. Myles Cosgrove.

As I approached the apartment, I could see a blue flickering light coming from the bedroom window from the television. The rest of the apartment was dark. We arrived at the door, and as I was preparing to knock, I saw Det. Hankison and Lt. Hoover's attention go to the upstairs apartment directly above our target location. I heard both officers giving commands for an individual to go back into his apartment. There was a loud exchange of both commands and the individual arguing with Det. Hankison and Lt. Hoover. This continued after I knocked on the target door the first time. The loud exchange was becoming a distraction to the task at hand, so I told Hankison to leave that alone and focus on what we were doing.

I was standing to the left of the door as I began to knock, something police are taught from day one in the academy since there have been many cases of subjects firing through doors when officers knock. Det. Nobles was to the right of the door holding the ram, a tool used to breach a door if there is no answer and that has been referred to as the "key to the city" since it has the uncanny ability to open most doors it encounters. Standing directly behind me was Tony (Det. James). Due to the small area we were dealing with, the additional officers on scene were to the right of the door.

We were all wearing black tactical vests that were issued by our department for this purpose with "POLICE" clearly stated on the front and back of our vests. This important point has been a topic of misinformation put out by the attorneys for Breonna Taylor's family. The news and social media outlets have taken this mistruth and run with it as an additional "botched" part of the raid, in some instances even painting the picture as if we were breaking into this apartment in plain clothes to avoid being identified as police. This narrative leads people to believe that we were not physically identified as police and leaves it open to an interpretation that we were doing something illegal. Nothing is further from the truth. Clear identification is a priority in any police function.

After the exchange with the upstairs neighbor was resolved, I continued knocking on the door. There's a knock known on the street as the knock of the police. It's not a typical knock that you would utilize when going to see a family member or friend. This knock is a loud, continuous pounding on a door. This knock is aggressive, forceful, and used this way with the purpose of obtaining a response. THIS is the knock we utilized on the fatal night of March 13, 2020. But it's not the only tool we used to get the occupants' response that night.

After using an open hand to bang on the door for two separate cadences with no response, I began to accompany each knock with a loud verbal announcement that we were the police and had a search warrant. Typically, we would use the Supreme Court's standard of giving the resident a reasonable amount of time before using the ram to breach the door. In this case we were asked to give Ms. Taylor *additional* time to get to the door, which we did. I banged on the door for the third time and yelled, "Police! Search warrant!" a couple of times. I waited a few seconds and banged again and repeated myself. After the fifth time banging and

third time yelling to the resident inside the house that we were the police, Det. Nobles stopped me. He said he thought he heard someone come up to the door. I then yelled, "Police! We have a search warrant! Open the door!" With no response, I banged one last time and announced our presence.

By this time, we had been knocking and announcing for forty-five seconds to a minute. This seems like an eternity when you are on the other side of an unknown threat. Imagine yourself at a red light at 3 a.m. with no cars in sight. The minute you spend sitting there waiting on the light to turn green feels like forever. Now take that feeling and amplify it by 100 when standing on the other side of a closed door you are preparing to go through. It was at this time I looked over my right shoulder to my lieutenant. He gave me the nod and said, "Let's hit it." I looked at Nobles and said, "Go ahead," not having any idea what we'd encounter on the other side of that door.

Mike prepared to ram the door. There's a common practice on warrants that becomes a habit. Regardless of who the point of contact at the door is, *everyone* announces "POLICE, SEARCH WARRANT" once the operator starts attempting to breach the door with the ram. I could hear the collective group announcing us over my own yelling that night. As police, we understand the reality that drug dealers get home-invaded at a much higher rate than the average citizen. With this in mind, we have no desire to have a shootout with someone who thinks they are being robbed. No one wins in that scenario.

I had the bird's-eye view to the ram placement on the door. I vividly remember the first strike hitting squarely on the deadbolt. This placement generally does not open the door, and this day was no different. While the lock bent, it did not give. The second strike to the door was solid, and the door came open enough where I could see through the frame and see the actual bolt bent. I remember making the statement, "This one is gonna do it. Here we go." The last strike exploded the door open with force. The door swung from right to left and gave me a clear view of the living room, which was positioned on the right side of the apartment. Mike stepped back out of harm's way on the right side of the door as to not be exposed to the "fatal funnel." The fatal funnel is the opening of a doorway that you must go through where you can be detected, but it's hard to identify your threat until it's too late. Reaction is always slower than action, so police are always at a disadvantage when going through the fatal funnel.

When the door opened, I could see everything to the right of the door in the living room including the color of the couches. I was still posted on the left side of the door frame, so my view was limited, and my body was concealed from the unknown threat inside. We were still announcing ourselves, as this practice is continued until the house is cleared of all threats. Again, this is to inform the residents that it is the police that are entering the dwelling. We WANT them to know it's us so that the very thing that happened doesn't. Our goal is to get in as safely as possible. I "sliced the pie" of the room. This is a technique that is used to clear as much of the room as you can from your current position of concealment or cover before over-committing to the unknown. In this case I was able to stay behind the door frame and clear the room from right to left before stepping in the threshold. I could identify there were no threats in the living room, but my visual real estate ran out once the doorframe and hallway wall came together in my view.

I had an idea of what the layout of the apartment was going to be due to the countless warrants I've been a part of over the years. The living room and kitchen are generally opposite of each other, and a hallway generally separates them down the middle. This apartment was no different, so my mind was telling me I'd encounter a hallway, but I'd need to go left to clear the dining room and kitchen. This is where the trust of your teammates comes in. I knew that, once I committed to go left, the detective behind me in the stack would follow me and cover the long hallway.

It's at this point that I was committed to moving forward. I always prefer being first in the door because I want to see what I'm encountering and have some control of my own destiny. I took a step forward with my left leg and then pivoted from left to right as I stepped in the threshold. I never made it in the apartment. No one did.

As soon as I stepped into the threshold, I saw two figures, approximately thirty feet away, lit up by the ambient light of the television coming out of the bedroom next to them and our flashlights. The next events took only a few seconds, but time slowed down, and my brain recorded so many of the details. The two figures were standing side by side at the end of the hallway, so close to each other that they could have been one, but I could see that one of the individuals was considerably taller than the other. That was the only defining difference in that millisecond. I couldn't tell if they were black or white, male or female. The taller figure, on the right, was stretched out in an "Isosceles Stance"—feet shoulder-width apart and both arms extended. My eyes fixated on the barrel of the 9mm semi-auto handgun that the man I now know was Kenneth Walker had outstretched. By the time my mind registered it was a gun, I saw the flash, heard the bang, and felt the smash to my thigh simultaneously. The bullet had ripped through the wallet in my front pocket and penetrated my thigh. It was like a piercing hot rod going through my leg.

Things happen so quickly in scenarios like this that you don't have time to reassess, and the only option for de-escalation is returning fire to keep the suspect from continuing to shoot at you. You don't have time to formulate a new plan. You simply react and revert to your training. I was able to, almost simultaneously, get off four rounds toward the immediate threat.

When my thigh was shot and the bullet ripped through the muscle, the left leg muscle stopped functioning, and my leg was operating on bone and tendon leaving it unstable and weak. My body drifted to the left, and I knelt down behind the door frame. I presented myself around the corner and placed two shots into the door jamb behind which Kenneth had hidden—I was trying to keep him from returning additional fire so I could get to safety and treat my wound. All this activity occurred within a few seconds at most.

Myles, who was behind me and flanking my right shoulder, bravely stepped up as I was going down and addressed the threat. He used his body as a shield and stepped on me to try to protect me, not knowing how gravely I was injured. I grabbed my thigh and felt a handful of hot blood. I've seen enough wounds and had enough first aid training to know this was serious. I yelled out, "I've been shot. It hit my femoral." I was sitting on my right hip with my left leg extended.

At this point tunnel vision started to kick in. I remember hearing gun fire, but things started closing in, and it began to get quiet. I remember thinking, *I've really been shot.* I extended my right hand, which contained my gun, across the concrete and let go of my gun for a brief second. My left hand was still holding pressure on my thigh. I shook my head back and forth to regain my composure. Training taught us that in order to shake off the tunnel vision you needed to move your head and keep your eyes moving. I was determined I wasn't dying here and like this. I mustered enough strength to get to my feet and began hobbling toward the parking lot, not knowing if I would get caught in the crossfire. At this point I couldn't tell who was shooting or where it was coming from. I just knew I was of no use and needed to get to cover and address my wound.

From this point on, I no longer had eyes on what was happening in the apartment. As I passed behind Myles, I looked to my left and could see Nobles trapped under the stairwell. I continued to hobble to the parking lot. I stepped off the curb between the first two cars I came upon. Out of habit I placed all my weight on my left leg as I stepped off the curb. My leg was having none of that and gave out on me. As I fell to the ground, I was met by Det. Campbell who was between the cars. My first thought was that he had been shot. We made eye contact, and I realized that wasn't the case. During that same moment I could hear another barrage of gunfire. Later I would find out that, on the heels of Cosgrove firing his weapon, Hankison had moved his position to the front of the apartment where the sliding glass door is. Brett didn't realize I had made it to safety, and by hearing the echoes from the gunfire by Cosgrove, he thought we were being executed by the suspect(s) inside the apartment. During this brief, yet chaotic moment, it's logical for Brett to have come to that conclusion.

As quickly as I heard the second volley of gunfire, it was over and was silent. I had scooted on my butt to the end of the car at this point. Suddenly, I was being dragged by my vest from behind and to safety by Lt. Hoover. I looked at him and said, "I need a tourniquet!" Lt. Hoover was scrambling and took his belt off in an attempt to stop the bleeding.

Nobles and Tony James had come running up at that point. I said, "Where is EMS? They were just down the street." I could hear people talking on the radio and requesting cars and asking for EMS. At one point I tried using my radio, but there was too much radio traffic and I kept getting cut out. I heard Brett call out that there was someone inside with a rifle. I yelled from my back that all I saw was a handgun, not a rifle. Nobles and Hoover were over me. Nobles tried pulling the belt tighter, but the leather belt was covered in blood, which made it impossible to grip and pull tight. Someone again yelled for a tourniquet. As I lay on my back on the wet asphalt, Hoover was kneeling on my left side and Nobles on my right. Both were giving me words of encouragement and telling me to hold on. I kept assuring them I was fine even though I wasn't convinced myself.

Suddenly, I saw Tony James come running up in front of me with a tourniquet in his hand that he had stowed in his vest. He handed it to Hoover who began to go to work. The pain I was experiencing wasn't so much at the point of the bullet entry but rather deep in my groin area and lower left side of my back, almost to the outer top of my hip. I thought maybe the bullet hadn't passed through my body and was lodged in my groin because, any time my leg was moved, the pain in my groin area was unbearable. Hoover lifted my leg to place the tourniquet on, and I gritted my teeth and moaned in pain. He apologized but kept his composure and focus. As he pulled the tourniquet tight around my leg, it lifted my leg. Nobles had to place his foot on my thigh while Hoover pulled it tight. It felt as though he was tearing my leg in half.

At this point I could hear the sirens from the responding patrol cars. The map showed two points of entry into the complex. However, the first entrance was divided from a subdivision by a ten-foot locked gate. The responding officer approached the first entrance and was met by the gate. I could hear Brett talking to the officer on the radio. Suddenly, Hoover yelled,

"Tell him to ram the gate!" In the movies, you ram your car through a gate, and it majestically flies open. Well, this wasn't the movies. The patrol officer rammed the gate, and the gate just folded down. It ripped the lights off the top of his car and the spotlight off the patrol car along with other damages, but the vehicle was able to get through, nonetheless.

I remember someone yelling for a knife to cut my pant leg off to make sure the tourniquet was above the wound. The patrol officer produced a knife and also had a blood clot kit and bandage. Hoover cut my pant leg off and looked to make sure things were positioned correctly. Nobles was squeezing my hand and telling me to talk to him and not shut my eyes. At this point I and several others were questioning where EMS was. These guys were just a couple of minutes away on standby but had yet to be seen. Hoover began applying the clot kit and bandage. They had to keep repositioning my body and leg to get the bandage wrapped properly. The pain was intense, but it was probably what kept me alert.

While they were working to get the bleeding under control, I suddenly had a thought. I couldn't let someone else call or wake my wife up. It would freak her out, and she would think I was dead. I pulled my phone out of my vest pocket and attempted to call Nicki. Nobles grabbed my phone and told me they'd take care of that and that I needed to focus on this.

I could hear the sirens and commotion in the background as officers were attempting to set up a perimeter and call the occupants of the apartment out. There's no way at this point, a few minutes after the initial incident, that Kenneth Walker didn't know it was the police outside, yet he chose to stay inside the apartment for fifteen minutes before exiting, claiming he didn't know who we were.

By now even more time had passed, and EMS still was nowhere to be found. Someone suggested that they put me in a car and take me to the hospital. I knew that University of Louisville hospital, the only hospital with a trauma care unit, was a good twenty minutes away. I also knew for a fact that EMS was still on standby and should be there any second. I overrode the recommendation and told them I wanted to wait for EMS. Had we been closer, and if I hadn't needed immediate lifesaving attention, then I would have been on board for that decision.

There was a moment where I could hear the people around me talking, and in my mind, I thought I was coherent. It was almost like a dream.

My body was trying to go into shock. Then I heard Nobles yell at me and squeeze my hand. "Stay with me! Say something!" That snapped me back to reality.

Just a short time later I heard someone say EMS was there. I was relieved, but then I heard them say EMS couldn't get through the downed fence. So Myles pulled his car up and the plan was formulated to drive me down to EMS. I heard Myles yell, "Put him in the trunk since he can't get in the back seat." I said I wasn't going in the trunk, to just shut it and I'd sit on it. Two officers carried me and sat me up on the trunk where I held on to the hard antenna that was positioned at the back of the roof.

While on the way toward EMS, I see the young white EMS technician walking toward us with his bag over his shoulder. I looked at the EMS rig and saw it start to pull off. I yelled, "Tell him to stop, we are coming!"

The young worker said, "I tried and he's not answering the radio."

I yelled back, "Get on your radio and try again!" Suddenly the rig stopped and pulled back up to the gate. I felt some relief, but my worst fears were coming true. This young and inexperienced crew, no matter how good their intentions, were going to hold my life in their hands.

Once we got as close to the gate as we could, Hoover told me to hang on and swooped me up in his arms like he was carrying a new bride over a threshold. I weighed 205 pounds and had an additional 25–30 pounds of gear on, so this was no easy task. He carried me about twenty feet and had to climb over the fence. He then carried me around to the back of the ambulance. The EMS driver opened the back door and started to pull the gurney out. I remember reaching out and grabbing ahold of the gurney and pushing it back in saying, "We do not need this now, I'm here." I climbed into the back of the ambulance, positioned myself on the gurney, and looked at Hoover. Seeing the look of exhaustion and concern on his face and hearing his deep breathing, I knew he was spent. He had just played a major role in saving my life. But I wasn't out of the weeds yet.

CHAPTER 5

MY GUARDIAN ANGELS AND ROOM 9

The other EMS worker climbed in the back of the ambulance. Right behind him, Tony James jumped in and closed the door. For about five seconds, everyone stood around and looked at each other, not knowing what to do. Tony addressed the two EMS workers and said, "What do you need me to do? Do you want me to drive?" The young, white kid said he'd drive and disappeared to the front of the ambulance. As I laid there on my back, I watched another EMT stand there with a confused look, clearly unsure what to do.

Tony again asked, "What can I do? How can I help?"

The young worker simply said, "I can't find my large gauze."

It was at this moment that I looked at him and said, "Am I your first gunshot wound victim?"

He knelt down by me and said, "To be honest, yes, you are."

I responded, "Well, this is the first time I've been shot, so let's not screw this up." I remember hearing the beep from the ambulance going in reverse, but the ambulance was barely moving. I was thinking, *What are we doing and why are we going so slow?*

Suddenly, the ambulance stopped, and the back doors swung open. It was like the gates of heaven swung open and the bright lights came in. Climbing into the back of the ambulance were two Pleasure Ridge Park firefighters who were paramedics. The first person I saw said, "I didn't expect it to be you."

My response was, "I'm glad it's you!" Josh Johnson was that paramedic. I've known Josh for a long time. I knew he was capable and competent.

He and his partner told the EMT to get out of the way and instantly went to work. They began vitals, both ran IVs and, more importantly, took control of the situation. I took off my vest, belt, and gun and took my wallet out of my front pocket. Tony took control of those items for safekeeping. I had no idea at this point that the bullet had traveled through my wallet before entering my leg.

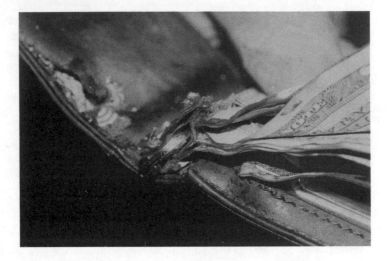

The EMS worker asked the paramedics what he could do. Josh instructed him to just record the times and what medicines were administered. I remember getting my first dose of fentanyl. It did absolutely nothing for the pain. Josh looked at me and said, "I hate to do this to you. You are gonna hate me, but I have to tighten this tourniquet more. You are still bleeding." I didn't realize it could go any tighter due to the amount of pain and pressure coming from it. He cranked it even tighter until the bleeding stopped. The pain was so intense it raised me up off the gurney.

At this point I knew I was going to live, but I didn't want to lose my leg. I knew from first aid courses that blood supply can only be restricted for so long before it causes permanent damage. This tourniquet had been on for a while now, and it was taking forever to get to the hospital. Imagine taking a rubber band and twisting it around your finger until you can't anymore. The finger will change colors and feel as if the skin around it is going to burst. The pain is intense, and you can't bend it. Now do that to the largest appendage on your body and leave it that tight for 35–40 minutes. I told Josh I needed more pain meds, so he administered morphine since the fentanyl hadn't touched the pain. Josh did his best to create small talk, and we even cracked a few jokes to keep the focus off the pain.

When we pulled up to U of L hospital, I knew I'd be going into Room 9. This is the best trauma unit in the region. They treat gunshot, stabbing, and car wreck patients multiple times a day. The STAT Flight helicopter brings patients here from all over for trauma care. If anyone can save you, it's Room 9. U of L is also a training hospital, so not only do you see the best doctors, but you are also observed by the up-and-coming doctors and nurses.

As they wheeled me in through the automatic doors, I could see a semi-circle of about 25–30 people around the bed watching the doctors as they began to work. Most looked young and the majority female. Why does this matter, you ask? Well, I knew what was coming next. The only thing I had left on my entire body was the upper portion of my pants that they couldn't cut off because they were trapped under the tourniquet. Suddenly, *all eyes on me* took on a whole new meaning.

As the doctor positioned the scissors to cut off the tourniquet, he was cutting toward my groin area. I said, "Be easy, Doc. There's not much room for a mistake." That lightened the mood up a little. Before he cut it off, they retrieved another tourniquet in case the bleeding became uncontrollable.

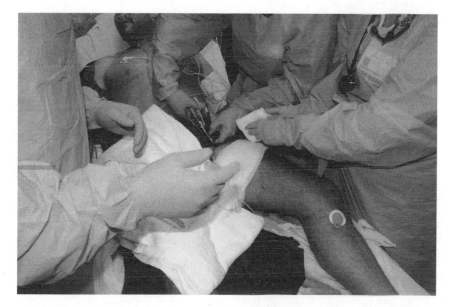

By this time, I had lost quite a bit of blood and was feeling lightheaded, and my skin tone was gray. The pain was still intense, so they gave me another round of fentanyl. While it didn't do a lot for the pain, it made me not care as much about it. Once the tourniquet was cut off, the doctor began to cut off what remained of my pants.

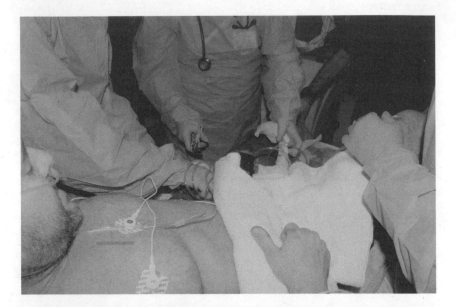

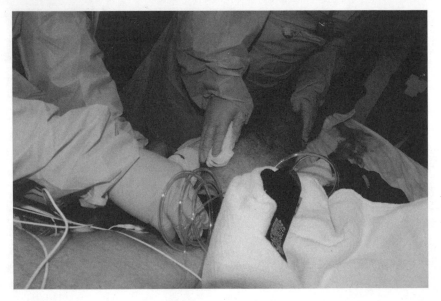

As the team examined me, they were looking for an exit wound. They flipped me back and forth on the bed several times and couldn't find the exit wound. Each time they moved me was extremely painful.

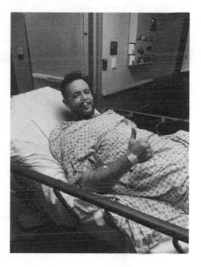

No one from my family had made it to the hospital at this point, and I didn't want them to worry any more than I knew they already would. My major, Kim Burbrink, was in Room 9 during this time, and as they were wheeling me to the CT scan, I asked her to take a picture and send it to my family. I mustered up a smile and a thumbs-up and proceeded to the scan.

The scan showed nothing foreign in the body. Once again, they searched my body for the exit wound before someone noticed an opening in the fold between my thigh and butt cheek where the bullet exited my body. This was somewhat relieving to hear because I still thought it was lodged up in my groin area due to the intense pain and hematoma that had formed. I was taken back to get an additional scan before they prepped me for surgery. By this time all the pain meds were kicking in, and I was getting a little fuzzy.

Getting ahold of my wife proved to be a little tricky. They tried calling Nicki's phone, but she happened to have it on silent that night. We'd sold our house in January of 2020 and were staying at a friend's house in her basement until we could finalize buying a new place. My police buddies Kevin, Daryl, and Steve—the sergeant who took my spot in the Major Case unit—knew we were staying at a friend's house, but they weren't sure exactly where. Through some detective work, and with the help of my friend Robbie, they finally reached the right residence. It was at this point that my wife received the news that is every police spouse's worst nightmare.

Kevin told her to get dressed and come with them. He told her I had been shot but that I was alive. She didn't remember most of the ride to the hospital because she was in shock. She was able to call my dad and oldest daughter and tell them what was going on. My oldest then called my other two adult children and filled them in. They were halfway to the hospital when Major Burbrink sent the picture with the thumbs-up to Kevin, and he was able to share that with Nicki. That picture at least let them know I was alive.

My heart was full to see my parents, wife, children, and sisters. I vaguely but fondly remember the hugs and sentiments of love.

The surgeon entered the room and explained that the femoral artery had been damaged and he would have to remove a section and replace it with a vein that he'd strip from another area of the leg.

The next thing I knew, I was waking up in the intensive care unit. When my eyes opened, I was staring at a manual clock, and it was 7:30 a.m. on the dot. The surgery took five hours, but it felt as if I had simply closed my eyes and opened them.

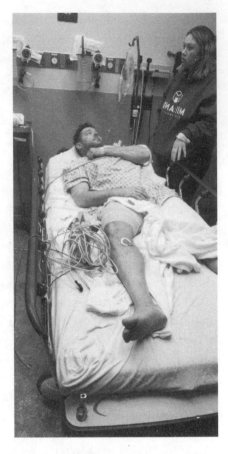

The thing that amazed me the most was how clear my recollection of the events from the incident were in my head. I could remember exactly what I saw: how many rounds I fired, what I said to people on scene. I wish I could have given my statement right then and there so all the naysayers couldn't accuse us of a cover-up and collusion like they have. I realize this isn't how everyone's body reacts to a traumatic injury like this, but mine did. There were a couple things I didn't recall, like putting on my ball cap before the raid, but most everything else was etched in my mind like a recording.

I did have one question though: Had anyone in that apartment died? I can't remember who told me the circumstances, but I felt horrible when I learned that a young, black female had been standing next to Kenneth (the shorter figure I'd seen in the hallway) and had been fatally shot. My head was spinning and I was sick to my stomach. This was a horrible tragedy and the exact scenario that every cop fears. As I lay in the hospital bed thinking about the events that had taken place, I remember telling my wife I wish I could ask Kenneth Walker some questions. I would ask him why Breonna was standing right there next to him. *Why so close? Why put her in harm's way if you truly thought we were intruders? Why leave her in the hallway while you jumped to safety after you fired the shot that hit me?* The WHY is what has plagued my mind. None of it made sense in that moment, and none of it makes sense now.

No one had to die that night. No one had to get injured. We went above and beyond to get someone, *anyone*, to answer that door. We went against our training and logic and gave those inside the opportunity to formulate a plan, believing our job is to preserve life, not take it. People across the world have accused us of being judge, jury, and executioner that night. There is nothing further from the truth. Once we were fired upon, we simply turned into self-preservationists. I've seen too many dead bodies, heard the screams of shattered family members, held and consoled mothers and fathers whose children have died. Police are not in the business of murder, and the accusations and assumptions about who I am and who my partners were that night are nauseating.

The next few days consisted of many visitors. Police officers, friends, and even a couple people I didn't really know came to show support. One that sticks out is a Secret Service agent whose family owns a local bakery. I'd love to mention the name, but I'm afraid they would be attacked. He brought up a couple boxes of their famous donuts. They are seriously the best donuts in town. Plus, I'm a cop and, well you know the rest. Anyway, he brought these donuts up the morning I came out of surgery. I was restricted from eating, so everyone else enjoyed the donuts but me, but the thought meant the world. The outpouring of support and love was amazing at first. The chief, whom I've not always agreed with but always respected, and the mayor, who is an opportunistic self-serving politician, came to the hospital to show support along with one of the assistant chiefs. It's amazing that as long as the media and woke mob aren't hounding you, you have politicians' support, but as soon as the tide turns and it's not in their best interest, they disappear never to be heard from again. I'll discuss this in more depth later in the book.

I stayed in intensive care for a couple more days then moved to a regular room. Every one of the hospital staff was amazing, from the doctors all the way to housekeeping. I didn't experience one negative look or word from anyone. At times I was allowed more guests than I should have been given the coronavirus pandemic just taking off, but they were all accommodating. I was able to leave the hospital on March 16, 2020, after three days. I left with little fanfare, which is what I wanted, just myself, my wife, and a couple friends. I just wanted to go home—even though I didn't have a home to go to since we were staying with friends.

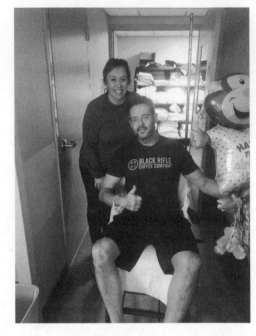

I know the Lord was looking over me that night. My faith lies in Him, and when it's my time to go, He will take me. My faith is the reason I've never been scared to die on this job. I know I'm in His hands, and I'm good with that. While death doesn't scare me, I don't want to leave my family behind, so it is nice to feel as though I have some guardian angels. My partners were my guardian angels that night as well as Josh and Rachel from PRP Fire. But there was one more person looking over me that night that I've never met and wish I could have. My wife's father passed away from cancer when she was a small child. Why is that relevant you ask? He died on March 13. I think he's looking down over us as any protective father would and knew this date would be another heartbreak to his daughter that he didn't want her to endure. Is this scriptural? Probably not, but God uses many tools to remind us He is in charge, and when she pointed out the significance in the date, it sent chills down my spine.

CHAPTER 6

THE CALM BEFORE THE STORM

We decided to stay at my parents' house since I couldn't climb up and down stairs. I was excited to spend some time with my parents, and my parents seemed just as thrilled. Life was different. I was used to working 60-plus hours a week, and now I was sitting around feeling as though I was wasting my days. However, the nights were filled with playing various games with my mom, wife, and sister.

My mom has always been a kid magnet. She loves them and they love her. She's just Nana to everyone. It's been this way my whole life. All the kids in church loved her growing up. She helped me teach my older kids how to ride a bike years ago. Now she's in her mid-seventies but still as spunky as ever. I hobbled outside one day in early April to see her teaching my then five-year-old how to ride his bike with no training wheels. Had this horrendous tragedy not taken place, I'm not sure my son would have this opportunity with his Nana.

The time with my family has been the silver lining in all this. We aren't getting any younger, and I now have memories and experiences I never would have had before. However, the negative spotlight, threats, and stress has taken its toll on all of us, especially on my parents—that is an additional burden.

The weeks that followed were life-changing for all Americans, not just for those involved in this tragic incident. COVID-19 had taken center stage, and businesses were beginning to shut down. We were getting daily updates on the virus, and none of it looked positive. However, the pandemic kept our incident out of the national spotlight. I was okay with that because I've been around this business long enough to know how narratives get twisted. I knew the fact that I am a white police officer and

Breonna Taylor was an unarmed black female gave this tragedy all the dynamics to explode into something it wasn't, something race-driven. In today's society, there's nothing the media salivates over more than a good black/white narrative. It pushes ratings and increases their bottom line.

Getting around was a daily struggle, but with each day I was getting stronger. Ice packs and ibuprofen had become my new best friends. I had a few in-person physical therapy sessions, and then due to the pandemic, they wanted to do virtual sessions. I opted out and chose to conduct the exercises on my own. A meal train was graciously set up by some police wives, and it was a huge blessing to me and my family. The Louisville Metro Police Foundation has been a huge support. I also received mail from people I had never met, sending me words of encouragement. All in all, things were good, considering the circumstances.

During this time, we purchased the perfect house for our family. It had all the little things we were looking for. It was a walkout ranch with a large garage positioned on a cul-de-sac in a quiet neighborhood. The neighbors were friendly, and there were other children in the neighborhood for our youngest to play with. We were out of Jefferson County and in a school district that we were excited for our son to attend. Houses were being sold well above market value within hours of being put on the market, so we were ecstatic when our offer was accepted and felt blessed to have secured this house. The bonus factor was that it was in close proximity to my parents and adult children. It was a win-win.

In late April we received the keys to the house and began moving things in. I was pretty much a lame duck and felt completely useless. The guys I worked with got together and graciously moved all my belongings. I'm not sure there's any greater proof of love than being willing to help someone move. Everyone despises it as it's not an easy task. I *hate* asking for help, but these brothers didn't bat an eye to carry the load for me.

We spent the next few weeks unpacking boxes and getting acclimated to our new living quarters. This was both exciting and overwhelming. Our son was thrilled to get his toys out of storage, and my wife and I were enjoying some much-needed privacy since we had been homeless for four months. The weather was getting warm, and the flowers were starting to bloom. We were getting to know our neighbors, and our son began to ride his bike and meet new friends. I began to gain strength back in my leg and was actually able to play with my son and grandson. I was still having knee and shoulder issues from the fall, but I was encouraged with the progress being made. Things started to feel normal again.

Although Breonna Taylor's family had filed a lawsuit in which their lawyer made some outlandish allegations, things were fairly quiet. A small group of her family members and friends would gather and demand justice. This group of individuals was not rioting. They were not stopping traffic. They were not causing damage to others' property. They were a group of heartbroken family and friends who wanted answers. I don't blame them because I would want the same. Little did I know that they were not being communicated with by the department. As tough as those conversations may have been to have, I do believe they deserved that. I experienced this same treatment later on, so I know the frustration, anger, and bitterness that comes from being shut out of what should be afforded you.

On May 11 nationally known civil rights attorney Ben Crump was hired as part of the legal team to bring attention to the case. Crump was already in the national headlines as the attorney representing the family for Ahmaud Arbery, who was killed on February 23 in Georgia. Crump made his usual rounds on national television making false and slanderous allegations about the events of March 13 and the officers involved. He started the false narrative that Breonna Taylor was asleep in her bed when she was killed. He said we didn't knock or announce and in fact he claimed we changed our story from no-knock to knock and announce to fit our narrative. He claimed they called 911 as we were busting the door down, which is an absolute lie. I'll go into the timeline later. He said we were in plain clothes, which is true, but it's misguided because he leaves out the fact we were clearly identified as POLICE with raid vests. Crump claimed we were at the wrong house and the suspect we were looking for was already in custody: 100 percent lies. He started the slogan, *If you run for Ahmaud, run for Breonna*, referring to the 2.23 miles people were encouraged to run in remembrance of Ahmaud and to fight racial injustice. Crump is very good at tying tragedies and injustices together to skew the narrative and hype up a crowd. That's why so many people believe that Trayvon Martin and Ahmaud Arbery were black men killed by white police officers. Both are not factual, but when they are combined with police tragedies over and over, people who are ignorant of the facts believe it's true.

When these lies were put out on national media outlets like MSNBC, *The View*, and many others, it's easy to see why so many people were outraged by what they perceived to be police misconduct. We were all brought up to believe the media was an unbiased news source where we could go to get the truth on stories. My, how things have changed. It was at this point the local media began to jump on the bandwagon. While my young son knew I had been shot, we tried to keep him shielded from the specifics of the case.

One day my son came in from playing outside. It was right around dinner time, so the TV show that had been playing went off and the local news came on. I heard him yell for his mom and me, so I came into the living room. He said, "Why is Daddy on TV?" The local news was running one of what would be countless stories with pictures and names of the officers involved plastered on the screen. We shuttled him back outside, explaining it was just about Daddy getting shot, and looked at each other in disbelief. From that moment on, there wasn't a time we turned the TV on, whether it was local or national news, that didn't touch on the story in some aspect.

Right after the story broke nationally, our social media pages began to get attacked. No one in the family was off limits. My adult children received hate and death threats as well as myself and my wife. Some were veiled threats, and others were detailed. All of our social media was shut down, and the family was shaken. As a father, I was infuriated. If you want to come after me, do so, but my family played no part in this. My family is made up of multiple races and ethnicities: white, black, and Chilean. As I mentioned earlier, we were raised in an inner-city church where everyone was welcomed and loved. We were taught the teachings of Christ, which are all inclusive. My son-in-law is black, and my grandkids are bi-racial, so when the narrative being spun was one of white supremacy and racism, I was appalled.

I remember the day I was at my daughter and son-in-law's house. We were sitting on their couch, and I asked him if he had received any grief from family or loss of friendships over all the media coverage. He told me a few friends had concerns and questions. My advice to him, and later to all my friends and family, was to remember that only one side was being put out by the media. I asked that they give their friends some slack because we've all been conditioned that, if it's on the news—especially repeatedly from many sources—that it must be true. I didn't want my situation to be the cause for loss of friendship or family divides. I believe in open dialogue and honest conversations. I also believe in giving people the benefit of the doubt. I've been on the other side where I believed what I heard about someone only later to find out I was given false information. We've all lost friends from this situation, and unfortunately the jury is still out on a few.

On May 18 Chanelle Helm of Black Lives Matter Louisville posted online the addresses, phone numbers, and emails of the officers involved in the case. "Doxing" is the new way to intimidate and encourage violence on people without directly making a threat, and no one holds these people accountable. The ironic thing is, later in the summer, she tweeted how inappropriate it was to give out her personal phone number to people requesting their bond posted because it was dangerous. Hmmm. So, it's okay for her to put others in danger but not the other way around.

I worked hard on my rehab, and my leg was almost back to normal. On May 21, I had just arrived in Portland, Oregon to take care of some business,

Chanelle Helm   •••
2h · 🌐

So folks thought it was appropriate to give out my personal number to folks with higher bonds than $5K. Not only was it not funny, it was highly fucking dangerous to do so.

and my wife and son were home. There were rumors floating that Chief Conrad was going to announce his plan to retire at the end of June, and the rumor was that Deputy Chief Robert Schroeder would be the interim chief until one was appointed. Schroeder is the only person from the chief's office that had periodically reached out to me. I texted and asked if he was going to be my new chief. He didn't respond by text but called me about five minutes later. As soon as I answered, he said, "Can I call you right back?" He hung up, and that's the last I ever heard from him.

It wasn't twenty minutes later I received a call from the Deputy Commonwealth's Attorney assigned to the narcotics division. I knew something was up by the tone in his voice. He proceeded to tell me that they were dropping Kenneth Walker's charges of assault and attempted murder of a police officer. He told me how much he objected to the decision, but ultimately that decision rested in the hands of Tom Wine, the Commonwealths' Attorney. He promised he would do everything he could to re-indict him once they built a stronger case. I knew he meant well but that it would never happen. This was a punch in the gut. This man almost took my life, was responsible for Breonna Taylor's death in my opinion, had lied multiple times (including initially saying Breonna shot the gun, not him), and he was walking away scot-free.

I really didn't know what to say. I asked why Tom Wine didn't have the courage to call me since it was his decision. The answer was because this prosecutor knew me from narcotics. What could I say at this point? I hung up the phone in disbelief. It felt as if all the blood had gone from my head. I know how long we banged and how loud we yelled while at that door, but I also knew Walker's grimy defense attorney, who has gotten many guilty murderers off in Louisville, would make a case that Walker didn't hear us. Not one single person from upper command in the police department reached out. Right then I knew where they stood. They were not willing to put themselves in the line of fire for one of their own. It was crickets. Chief Conrad made a weak statement, but said he had faith in Wine and left it political.

I didn't have time to be upset for long. Less than an hour after the decision was announced on television, I received a call from my boss saying credible threats were beginning to come in from a confidential informant. These threats had specific names and methods and were coming from the leaders of two of the black motorcycle clubs in Louisville, No Haterz and STR8 RYDERS, known to the police for their alleged illegal activities. Breonna Taylor's mom is a member of one of the clubs, and her boyfriend is the president of that club. The informant said that the two clubs' presidents along with a couple members were devising plans on how to retaliate for Breonna's death and that a hit had been placed on the officers involved. At this point I was two thousand miles away from home on business and feeling helpless. My adrenaline was through the roof. I remember pacing the hallways of the hotel and making calls to all the contacts I could think of to get to the bottom of this. Kevin, once again, rushed to pick Nicki and my son up and take them to an undisclosed location until I was able to return home.

I rushed home, and we immediately shored up the security around the house. I was on high alert by then, but nothing had yet been corroborated about the threats. My family was able to come home thanks to Tom Schardein. He was one of the commanders of our dignitary protection team and a good friend and was able to get a security detail set up for the families. This was only the beginning of a long and exhausting journey.

Probably the most frustrating thing in all of this, up to this point, was the fact that, had the city or department simply refuted the lies that were being spread on a daily basis, the tragedies that lay ahead might have been prevented. Mayor Fischer and Governor Beshear had both been non-supportive and were playing a peculiar, passive-aggressive role against the police, adding to the hate and division that was starting to build. Both men kept saying they wanted to get justice for Breonna Taylor and that they wanted to honor her legacy. What does justice for Breonna even mean? The truth? Or revenge? The definition was never given by either, leaving it wide open to interpretation. Political and social pressures derailed any chance of real justice in this tragedy. I too had been shot, but I was ignored as a victim by the FBI, lost my career, lost money, had to sell my house, lost privacy, lost my freedom and my sense of security, lost sleep, been stressed, worried for my family's safety, been forced to leave town. All for doing the job that was asked of me that night.

On several occasions the Taylor family and their attorneys were given the official platforms of the mayor and governor and used those platforms to call us murderers and demand our termination and arrest. Several of the City Council members also called us murderers and said we assassinated Breonna. One even called Kenneth Walker a hero. There was never any pushback from anyone on my department. The Fraternal Order of Police (FOP) took a stance, but no one within the city's official rank did. The entire narrative was that three white cops conducted a botched raid and murdered an innocent black woman in her bed while sleeping and now were being protected by the system. When we called and begged police and city officials to correct the lies, we were told they didn't want to set precedent for future cases by commenting on ongoing investigations. This was a malfeasance by city leaders, particularly Mayor Fischer. This was not your typical run-of-the-mill case. This was a story that had picked up national attention and caused lives to be at stake. Unfortunately, this was just one of the many missteps the city would make with this case, and those mistakes caused a snowball effect of injustices that was just getting started.

Back on May 14, 2020, I could already feel the swell building. I didn't know to what degree, but the racial tension nationwide and anti-police rhetoric was building. I've said this before, and I'll proudly say it again; I love the city where I was born and raised. I've always been proud to be from Louisville and be a University of Louisville Cardinals fan. The last thing I wanted was my city in turmoil, especially over a false narrative, so I decided to contact David James, our City Council president.

To give a little background, David had also been a Louisville Police Officer for twenty years. While I was in the police academy in 2000, David was one of our main instructors. He was a good storyteller and had the uncanny ability to make everyone feel like his friend. I guess that made for a smooth transition to the world of politics after his policing career. David had been a narcotics detective before coming to the academy. His stories and excitement for working in narcotics left an impression on me as I already had an interest in that area. David reached out to me after I was shot and told me he was happy I was still among the land of the living. That meant a lot to me, so when I felt I was spinning my wheels trying to get someone from Metro Government to tell some truths, I decided I'd reach out to David. After all, he was the former FOP president and current president of Metro Council, and I knew he had aspirations to run for mayor after Fischer's term was up. Who better to set the ship straight and protect the city than the guy who wanted to be its next mayor? Boy, was I wrong!

Thirteen days *before* the first riot, and before the death of George Floyd, I sent a detailed text to David explaining all the lies and the potential problems this could create. I wanted to avoid, at all costs, trouble in our city. David told me he was going to hold a press conference to say all the things the mayor refused to say. But that press conference never happened.

CHAPTER 7

THE EXTRACTION

When the videos of George Floyd surfaced from Minneapolis, the entire country gasped. I remember getting calls and texts. My response was that this was bad, *really* bad. I remember every police officer I talked to about this disagreed with the way things were handled, at least with the limited information and edited videos we saw. Being right in the middle of a situation that was perpetuated based on lies and misinformation, I was careful not to play "Monday morning quarterback," but even with that in mind, it was hard not to accept what I saw. I knew that was NOT our policy on how to maintain control. Even if it were a tactic to gain control, I'd hope one would have enough common sense to reposition someone who was not an active aggressor or resisting. But having said that, someone who is high is difficult to keep under control, and their ability to process commands is impaired. The trial has yet to start while I'm writing this, so we don't have all the information, but my first thought was, *This guy will probably go to prison.*

The common denominator between both tragedies is Benjamin Crump. He seems to sniff out the national stories that can make him a buck, get some screen time, and gain him more notoriety. He gets on TV like a televangelist and piggybacks the tragedies these families are going through. Maybe his intentions are good, but telling the truth to go along with those intentions is something he's allergic to, evidently. You can't say you are fighting for justice while causing injustice to others along the way.

Now we had the Breonna Taylor tragedy sandwiched between two other divisive national news stories that involved black and white in which Crump is controlling the narrative and has free reins to the media.

These other cases were caught on camera, and both appeared to be injustices. The perfect storm was brewing, not only for Louisville, Kentucky,
but for America and across the world. We have media and social media
platforms that thrive off of divisiveness and hate. Americans will devour
their own for the sake of a like or share. Americans are now WOKE, and
you better be on their side or they will seek to destroy you. Myself and
my coworkers were now on that radar, and the mob was out to destroy us.

On May 28 the recording of Kenneth Walker calling 911 was released
to the media. In that phone call, you hear a person crying out that someone broke in and shot his girlfriend. The emotions sound real and could
pull at your heartstrings if you didn't know the entire story and the context of the call. The money-seeking attorneys that released the call knew
exactly what they were doing. If they manipulated the way the evidence
was released, then they would win the case in the court of public opinion.
When that happens, there is a better chance of an out-of-court settlement,
which means no additional discovery and depositions, which would have
shed light from the other side of the story.

There are just a few problems with the narrative that was attached
to the phone call and story surrounding it. This 911 call was placed *over
six minutes after* the fatal encounter with police. The lawyers and media
set up the narrative to imply that, while we were banging on the door attempting to make entry, Kenneth Walker called 911, not knowing we were
the police. The facts are that we knocked and announced for so long that
he had time to get dressed, obtain his firearm, and take a position in the
hallway waiting for us to enter. Once the door was breached, we *continued to announce ourselves* as the police—all *before* the encounter. None of
this was mentioned each time the call was shared on the news and social
media. It was deflating to watch and hear one side presented while gag
orders had been placed on us officers.[2]

Let me play devil's advocate for a minute. Let's say Walker didn't hear
us announce and thought we were breaking into his home. Let's say after
he shot me, he still didn't know we were the police. If that was indeed true,
then why didn't he call 911 during the minute the door was being banged
on? Why didn't he have his girlfriend hide while he addressed the per-

---

[2] For the full 233-page report of the investigation into the Breonna Taylor shooting, please see **http://www.louisville-police.org/DocumentCenter/View/1818/
PIU-20-019-Investigative-Reports.** This is all the information we weren't allowed to
share and that the media wasn't telling.

ceived threat? Breonna had a phone in her hands when the tragedy happened, so why wasn't she calling 911? Was she calling or texting someone else during the raid? That phone was locked and was never accessed to see its activity. Walker claims that, once fire was returned, after his "warning shot," that he threw his gun under the bed in the sister's room. Again, if he indeed did not know we were the police, then why in the world would he throw his only source of protection into another room? Walker claims he helped Breonna to the floor after she was tragically shot. Impossible. The bullet holes in the wall where he was originally standing would've struck him.

No. In reality, he shot his gun and dove to safety, leaving poor Breonna stranded in that narrow dark hallway. He waited over six minutes to call 911 and still claimed, implausibly, that he didn't know who was outside. Within a few minutes of the shooting, many marked units were outside the apartment with lights and sirens. And who calls their mother before 911 if they think they've just been home-invaded, watched the love of their life murdered, and could still hear the people that did it outside their apartment? All the while he claimed to be holding Breonna with his door wide open. The position of her body in the hall makes the scene he's described in his many interviews impossible. Lastly, who blames the love of their life as being the person who shot a cop so as to not incriminate himself? Who does that?? Logic and common sense combat all these lies that Kenneth Walker claimed.

There are recordings from jail just a few days after Kenneth lost the "love of his life." He was so torn up about it all that he was trying to convince the girl on the other end to have phone sex with him. A few days later, he was recorded telling another girl that he loved her and was going to marry her. That doesn't sound like a guy who was getting ready to propose to the love of his life. If so, he got over her pretty fast.

There are a lot of unanswered questions as to the phone calls made by Kenneth Walker before he surrendered. He was in that apartment for fifteen minutes after the initial incident. What was he doing that entire time? Was he flushing evidence? Was he staging his scene? Was he hiding an additional firearm, maybe the one he claimed Breonna shot? We've been accused of some outrageous claims, so I'd like to know the truth. He tells us, and phone records corroborate, that he called his mother, 911, and then Breonna's mother before surrendering with no blood on his body or clothes. Does that sound like someone who held Breonna's bloody body as she passed?

One very important interview that wasn't discovered until the investigation was over was with LMPD Officer Donavis Duncan, conducted by the Public Integrity Unit in May of 2020. Officer Duncan lived in the same apartment complex as Breonna Taylor. He also went to middle and high school with Kenneth Walker and is a self-admitted friend. He knows Kenneth's mother and came out of his apartment and to the scene after the shooting. He stated that Kenneth Walker's mother approached him on scene and said, "Kenneth called me and said they're at the door." She told Duncan that she replied, "Who's at the door, baby?" She stated that Kenneth responded, "The police. I don't know what they want." She said, "Then he hung up."[3] I don't know why this wasn't a point of interest during the investigation or weighed in before dropping the charges on Walker since it clearly points to the fact that Kenneth Walker KNEW the police were at his door.

Minnesota had already begun to boil over from George Floyd's death. The strategic timing in the release of the 911 call along with the manipulation of the events in the timeline caused Louisville to erupt. Ben Crump, Sam Aguiar, and Lonita Baker, all attorneys for Breonna Taylor's family,

[3] Interview with Officer Donavis Duncan, Public Integrity Unit, May 20, 2020, page 168 of the following report: http://www.louisville-police.org/DocumentCenter/View/1818/ PIU-20-019-Investigative-Reports?bidId=.

were using the media as their mouthpiece to propagate their narrative and raise tension levels in the city.

One of the main false statements made repeatedly by the attorneys is that the police were in on a cover-up because we murdered Breonna. The claim is asininc. Had any of us officers that were at the scene that night been devising a plan and a cover-up, we did a horrible job. If you listen to the interviews, each is given from a different perspective. It's kind of like the Gospels in the Bible—Matthew, Mark, Luke, and John. They all tell the

LOUISVILLE METRO POLICE DEPARTMENT
SPECIAL INVESTIGATIONS DIVISION
Public Integrity Unit
INVESTIGATIVE REPORT

Type of Investigation		File No.	Date of Report:
OIS		20-019	5/21/2020
Activity:		Submitted By	
Interview with Officer Donavis Duncan		Sgt. Amanda Seelye	
		Lead Investigator:	
		Sgt. Amanda Seelye	

Interview with Officer Donavis Duncan

On Wednesday May 20, 2020 at approximately 1900 hours, Sgt. Jason Vance from the Public Integrity Unit and I interviewed Officer Donavis Duncan at the Public Integrity Office located at 3672 Taylor Blvd. The interview was about the officer involved shooting incident occurring on Friday March 13, 2020 at 3003 Springfield Drive #4. The interview was nineteen minutes and twenty-nine seconds (19:29) in length. The following will be a brief synopsis of the interview. The complete audio file can be found in the case file.

Prior to the interview, a police officer recorded statement form and Miranda Rights waiver was completed. Officer Duncan was the courtesy officer at the apartment complex where the incident occurred on March 13, 2020. Officer Duncan has been the courtesy officer since November 2018. Officer was off work and at home when the incident occurred. His apartment was located in the front section as the involved apartment was located in the back section of the apartment complex. Officer Duncan cannot see the involved apartment from his apartment.
He heard between 15/20 shots and then the report of an officer involved shooting was dispatched on his police radio. Officer Duncan immediately ran to the scene and set up a perimeter at the corner of the apartment building at the request of an unknown Narcotics detective. He recalled hearing the suspect being hailed out of the apartment. Officer Duncan assisted with taping off the perimeter of the scene with police tape.

Officer Duncan spoke to the suspect's family who arrived on scene after it was secure. Officer Duncan was familiar with the suspect, Kenneth Walker, from attending the same high school. He was aware of Mr. Walker frequenting the apartment at 3003 Springfield Drive #4 but didn't know the female who resided at the apartment except knowing she was Mr. Walker's girlfriend from pictures on Facebook. Officer Duncan would see Mr. Walker from time to time in the apartment complex. Mr. Walker would ask Officer Duncan hypothetical police related questions. He did not communicate with Mr. Walker by phone or text message. He recalled Mr. Walker attended Western Kentucky University (WKU) at the same time as his girlfriend and he was aware of his involvement with marijuana.

Officer Duncan referenced being contacted by an Officer Garcia from the 2nd Division in 2019 about Mr. Walker and a homicide scene. Sgt Vance asked a couple follow up questions about this topic. Officer Duncan explained Officer Garcia told him a gentleman shot his girlfriend and the gentleman was a friend of Mr. Walkers. Officer Garcia alleged Mr. Walker removed something from the scene. Officer Garcia reached out to Officer Duncan because he lived in the same apartment complex as Mr. Walker. Officer Duncan stated he advised Mr. Walker to

Page 1 of 2

contact the police department regarding what Officer Garcia told him. He could not advise if he did contact the police or not.

Officer stated he spoke to Mr. Walker's family first on scene. He stated he knew his mother but not his father. Officer Duncan stated Mr. Walker's mother told him he called her. His mother stated Mr. Walker said, "they are at the door", him mother asked, "who is at the door" and Mr. Walker responded with "the police, and I don't know what they want", then the call ended. Officer Duncan stated what Mr. Walker's mom told him stuck with him because the information wasn't consistent with the reports from the media stating he didn't know who was at his door because he told his mom he knew it was the police. A little while later, Officer Duncan spoke to Breonna Taylor's family. Sgt. Vance told the family of Breonna's passing while Officer Duncan was standing there on scene.

Officer Duncan was requested by maintenance and the property manager to accompany them back to the apartment later in the day on March 13, 2020 to assist in securing the apartment and the other apartment involved in the incident.

Officer Duncan stated Mr. Walker could have his number in his contacts due to having the same phone number for many years and knowing him since high school.

Officer Duncan stated he had never been in the apartment before the day of the incident. Officer Duncan stated Mr. Walker was at the apartment very often. He would see Mr. Walker in the morning when he was coming home from work and when he would walk his dog he would see Mr. Walker's car in the parking lot. He believed Mr. Walker lived at the apartment and had been staying there even before November 2018. Officer Duncan did not know of any other males coming and going from the apartment.
The interview ended at 1917 hours with nothing further to report.

END OF REPORT

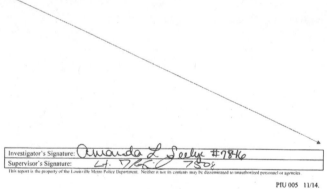

Page 2 of 2

same story but from different viewpoints, experiences, and perspectives. If we had devised a cover-up, wouldn't it be logical to think our stories would line up and there'd be no discrepancies? In our interviews there are variances because the recollection of events is different according to what stress each person was under, how individual bodies reacted to that stress, and what position they were in when the tragedy struck. This isn't an uncommon occurrence during chaotic stressful events. That's why eyewitness testimony is so unreliable. Studies have shown that almost seventy-five percent of false convictions are caused by an inaccurate eyewitness statement. What would be *uncommon* is if all seven officers had close to or identical statements. That would raise eyebrows amongst the professionals. There's no better evidence that we did not collude and conspire to cover up anything than our statements. The media was more than happy to take the attorneys' words at face value and spread the divisiveness. Nothing sells news like drama. Especially a black victim and a white cop. That is a media jackpot.

On May 28, 2020, my wife and I were lying in our bed watching what began as peaceful protests early in the evening quickly turning into chaos and illegal activities. Fires were being set, police vehicles damaged, rocks and bottles thrown at police. Buildings were being damaged. Suddenly, in a crowd of thousands of unruly people, shots began to ring out. When the shooting stopped, a total of seven people had been struck with gunfire. The very police who were being cursed and assaulted just moments earlier were now risking their lives to come to the aid of the citizens who had been shot. Even during this moment of bravery and self-service, the police officers were being berated and threatened. I watched in disbelief and anger at what I was seeing. I was sick to my stomach because I felt some responsibility for what these officers were enduring. I am a cop. These are my brothers, and I was of no use to them. SWAT took it upon themselves to put a patient in their BearCat [armored vehicle] and rush him to the hospital. Had they waited for EMS to get through the crowd, there was a good chance this victim would have bled out. The thanks these guys received was a lawsuit a few weeks later. The victim stated he was injured during the ride to the hospital because it wasn't an ambulance.

For the next four days I was glued to the television and social media. While watching the protests, the sweat would be running down my armpits from witnessing the chaos that was taking place in my city. After the first night, I began getting texts about people holding signs and wearing T-shirts with my name on them. Some wannabe artist even attempted, and failed, to spell my name.

I vacillated between a state of disbelief and anger at what I saw. It was like a dream. No, make that a nightmare. I watched as businesses were destroyed, livelihoods were taken away from people, and control of the city was completely lost because of weak city leaders. Protesters were get-

ting within inches of the police
officers' faces and screaming ob-
scenities, calling them murderers
and white supremacists. I've never seen this level of boldness and
disrespect against the police in my
twenty-year career. I was in constant contact with my friends on the department to make sure they were safe.

By the third night of the protests, the National Guard was called in to
assist. As the crowd broke up and shifted from downtown to the west side
of the city, the police response was forced to move as well. Mobs of people
were taking over streets and business parking lots. The business owners
as well as those in the community who were not taking a part in this unruly protest were now calling for police assistance.

There's a gas station and food mart on the corner of 26th and Broadway, and throughout my entire career, there have always been issues on
this lot. There were shootings, car-jackings, and drug dealing that took
place on a weekly basis. Across the street from this gas station was a small
business run by David McAtee. He had several meat smokers in the back-
yard and ran his business out of a converted shotgun house. Mr. McAtee
was known in the neighborhood for his delicious barbecue. Summer
nights you could ride down Broadway and smell the aroma of his grill-
ing consuming that block. He was a popular individual with people in
the neighborhood. Personally I had never heard anything negative about
him. For whatever reason on this night, something went terribly wrong.

As the police and National Guard moved in to clear out the lot in
the gas station, some individuals became unruly and began to threaten

the police. Pepperball guns were used to clear the crowd as the police felt they were being surrounded. A large number of individuals decided they were going to run in to Mr. McAtee's place of business, which had indoor and outdoor cameras. The video later released showed a group of people running through the back door and Mr. McAtee pulling out handgun. It appeared as though a female behind McAtee pulled at his shirt, trying to keep him from opening the back door and stepping outside. As police fired the pepper balls in the direction of the crowd and business, Mr. McAtee made the fatal error of opening his back door, stepping outside, and firing his gun toward the police and National Guard. Gunfire was returned by both an officer and a National Guard member. One of the bullets from the National Guard member's weapon struck David McAtee and killed him.

This incident poured fuel on a fire that was already burning like an inferno. The narrative once again was pushed that the police had shot an unarmed black man for absolutely no reason. A couple of days went by before the city agreed to release the video showing the actions of Mr. McAtee the night he was fatally wounded. The city had no plans on releasing this video, but someone on the inside told the media that there was a video of the incident. The media pressure forced the city's hand to do the right thing for once. This didn't diminish the effect that this incident had on the already volatile situation, but it kept the narrative from being spun any further, unlike in our case. It's sad that in both tragedies it took a leak from the department to the media to get some truth out.

I remember feeling as though a boa constrictor was around my chest and everyday got tighter and tighter. I did my best to downplay the threats to my family and be a rock for them, but I was growing concerned. My hyper-vigilance was beginning to consume me. Every car that passed the house was a threat. Going to the grocery store was now more of a protection detail than a family chore.

Sunday, May 31, I was attempting to organize my garage around ten o'clock at night to take my mind off the protest and distance my mind from the chaos for a few minutes. I received a phone call that would send my family and the other officers and families involved into a frantic mode of self-preservation. We already had security placed on our residences due to all the online threats and information received from two separate local informants. Then the FBI had been presented with the local threats due to their severity. They agreed to take the lead on the case because the informants came from two separate agencies, one from LMPD and one from ATF (Bureau of Alcohol, Tobacco, Firearms and Explosives). The informants did not know one another that we are aware of. They definitely didn't know each other as informants for law enforcement, yet the threats they brought to law enforcement corroborated the other's claims. Up to this point, I did not have any details of the threats, or how serious the FBI had concluded they were.

During the phone call, I was told I needed to get my family together immediately and relocate to an undisclosed location. This included any family members who were located in or around the Louisville area. I was told that officers from our Dignitary Protection Team were being sent to my children's locations until we could get them all together. I began to make phone calls to try and discern if this threat was as serious as was being related to myself and the others involved. A source within the FBI told a coworker of mine that, if it were his family, he'd take the advice and leave the city. Breonna Taylor's birthday was five days away on June 5. Part of the alleged threat was that those celebrating her birthday, with a balloon release, wanted to have something else to celebrate—that being revenge in the form of the death of one of the officers or a close family member. A $50,000 bounty had been placed on our heads.

My head was spinning. My adrenaline was pumping. How was I going to tell my adult children, parents, and siblings they had to pack up and come with me? I began making calls and explaining the best I could the dire situation we were in. I loaded my personal belongings along with guns and ammo. If I had my way, I'd have sent my family away and waited for the threat to show up, but I had to think in the best interest of my family. We gathered at a meeting point. It was like a scene out of the movies, but it felt like a nightmare I couldn't wake up from. We left Louisville, a caravan consisting of five carloads of family members and ten unmarked police vehicles with heavily armed and well-trained officers escorting us. A great friend and his family graciously allowed us to stay at their place far from Louisville. I'd love to give them the credit they are due, but I can't place them in danger as there has been no resolution to the threats.

It was after 3 a.m. by the time we got to our destination. As we unloaded the vehicles, there was an eerie silence. It was a combination of shock, fear, and disbelief. How did the situation go from a police officer being shot in the line of duty while attempting to get drugs off the streets that were killing people to that very cop being hunted for the fallout of that tragic event? As we got settled in that night, some of the officers that escorted us stayed for security purposes. This security detail lasted for months and potentially thwarted other perceived threats that occurred. I'm eternally grateful for the sacrifice and time away from their own families that these officers gave to protect mine. The weeks that followed were just the beginning of nationwide and worldwide hate directed at myself and the other officers involved that night.

CHAPTER 8

#SAYHERNAME

By early June, the #SayHerName #JusticeForBre #BreonnaTaylor hashtags were trending on all the social media platforms. Attached with those hashtags were pictures of the officers involved calling us murderers and demanding our heads on a stick.

Let's get something straight before I delve into this chapter. I have absolutely nothing negative to say about Breonna Taylor as a person. I had never met her and had never heard her name until the evening of the warrants. I'm sure she was an incredibly sweet person who was loved by many. The facts of her past involvements weren't discovered or put out by me. The facts surrounding a murder victim found in a car she rented was neither investigated nor dispensed by me. The facts of her involvement with Jamarcus Glover were put out on jail calls by Jamarcus Glover himself, not me. The fact that there is video of Breonna going to the trap house on Elliott Ave. with Jamarcus Glover was not put out by me. The fact that the investigators have photos of Jamarcus Glover picking up a package from her apartment was not created by me. The fact that Jamarcus Glover drove her car to do his dirty business and used her address as his on his driver's license and bank account isn't on me. So, while I have nothing bad to say about her, I also was not responsible for her life choices or the way those choices characterized her.

That being said, Breonna DID NOT deserve to die on March 13, 2020. Therefore, I have no problem with people saying her name. My wish would be to have that phrase put into context though. The #SayHerName hashtag movement was Launched in December 2014 by the African American Policy Forum (AAPF) and Center for Intersectionality and Social Policy Studies (CISPS), and the mission statement from www.aapf.org states, "The #SayHerName campaign brings awareness to the often-invisible names and stories of Black women and girls who have been victimized by racist police violence and provides support to their families." Their statement says that the hashtag is for who have been victimized by *racist police violence*. But Breonna's tragedy is NOT one of racist police violence. This tragedy is a culmination of events that led us to a raid on that apartment along with the criminal actions of Kenneth Walker that night, but that distinction was lost, or rather, buried.

Word hustling, influence-based bullying, and abuse of power to the utmost extremes was taking place. In a statement from the *Washington Post* article on August 18, 2020, attorney Benjamin Crump said he called "every Black female of influence" he knew, "including actress Tiffany Haddish and Sen. Kamala D. Harris (D-Calif.)," in an effort to get the word out and sway public opinion.[4]

Tamika Mallory and justice warrior group Until Freedom put out a call of action by releasing a video asking, "Do you know what happened to Breonna Taylor?" Several high-profile actresses and performers were featured posing this question before playing a short video full of mistruths about the events that night. The video claimed we were searching for two people who were already in custody. It was actually a search warrant for drugs, money, and evidence *tied* to Glover, not for Glover, and they were not already in custody. The warrants were served simultaneously. Second, the video says we did not knock or announce. Both of those statements are false. There's one thing that was said that I agree with. Tamika Palmer said she didn't want this to happen to anyone else. I agree, Tamika. I pray no one else has to lose a child senselessly. My twenty-five-year-old female cousin just passed from an overdose from the poison being spread by these same types of criminal organizations. So, I also want to keep that kind of loss from happening to any other parent because their lives have been torn apart as well.

The story then transitions into Tamika Mallory with her call to action on who to contact and what demands to give, specifically all-inclusive demands for justice because anything less was unacceptable and considered a miscarriage of justice and white supremacy. This video went viral.

---

4   Josh Wood and Tim Craig, "As Breonna Taylor protests stretch into 12th week, calls for officers' arrests intensify," *Washington Post*, August 18, 2020, https://www.washingtonpost.com/national/as-breonna-taylor-protests-stretch-into-12th-week-calls-for-officers-arrests-intensify/2020/08/18/ce6f2b9a-d823-11ea-930e-d88518c57dcc_story.html.

Alicia Keys's single Instagram post received over 2.4 million views—one person on one social media platform influencing over 2.4 million people with mistruths. Just about every well-known movie star, actress, and music performer with influence posted this video on their Facebook, Twitter, and Instagram pages. It was viewed and shared by tens of millions of people. Their mission was completed, heart strings were pulled, and the narrative was set on a worldwide scale.

aliciakeys ✓   ...

2:38

Watch IGTV Video   Alicia Keys

♡ ○ ◁   ⊓

2,447,604 views

aliciakeys Justice For Breonna Taylor · Do you know what happened to #BreonnaTaylor? The officers John Mattingly, Brett Hankison and Myles Cosgrove who took part... more

View all 2,909 comments

arrowbenjamin 🙏

mashondatifrere 🙏 🙏 🙏 🙏

June 10, 2020

Oprah Winfrey, probably one of the world's most recognizable names, joined the fight.

Winfrey wrote, "Today would've been Breonna Taylor's 27th birthday. But she's not here to celebrate, because shortly after midnight on March 13 Louisville police entered her apartment unannounced [FALSE]—and after a brief confrontation with her boyfriend [I think she meant when he shot a police officer], shot her eight times. The officers have not been fired or charged."

Winfrey continued by remembering Taylor as an "award-winning EMT" [she was only an EMT for five months with no awards] who "doesn't even get to celebrate her birthday."[5] While I was disgusted, I did have to consider the source. This is the same person who had recently said during her show, "There are white people who are not as powerful as the system of white people—the caste system that's been put in place. But they still, no matter where they are on the rung or ladder of success, they still have their

---

5 John P. Wise, "Oprah Winfrey posts about Breonna Taylor," WAVE 3 News, June 5, 2020, https://www.wave3.com/2020/06/05/oprah-winfrey-posts-about-breonna-taylor/.

whiteness." Oprah then said that white people have a "leg up" and added, "You still have your whiteness. That's what the term 'white privilege' is. It means that whiteness still gives you an advantage."[6] This statement was true in the days of slavery and Jim Crow, but this was 2020 and came from a woman of color who had a horrendous upbringing at the hands of her own but managed to succeed. She overcame her challenges by becoming a billionaire with the same opportunities we are all afforded. So, her opinion means nothing to me, but her far-reaching influence is troubling because we live in a world of reality with real consequences. Radicals will take these lies and contorted truths and act out in unpredictable ways.

In August, an article by CNN was headlined, "Oprah's O Magazine puts up billboards all over Louisville demanding action in the Breonna Taylor case."[7] In fact, twenty-six billboards were placed all around Louisville and paid for by *O, The Oprah Magazine.*

The following month, Breonna Taylor was the first person, besides Oprah, to be featured on the cover of her magazine. Oprah has now given more credibility to the group Until Freedom and all the hate that Tamika Mallory and her cronies spew.

I'm 100 percent against racism of any sort, and to falsely accuse someone of such a heinous and immoral trait is nothing short of character assassination. At what point is someone's reputation irrevocably damaged due to millions of people repeatedly hearing and sharing lies about them? Mark Twain is credited with the phrase, "A lie can travel halfway around the world while the truth is putting on its shoes." In this day and age of the internet and social media, a lie can be spread to millions by pressing send on your phone. Once that lie is out, it's virtually impossible to stop the spread.

Oprah is just one example of hundreds: LeBron James, Cardi B., George Clooney, Beyoncé, Common, Kim Kardashian, Alicia Keys, Demi Lovato, Ellen DeGeneres, Amy Schumer, Ice Cube, Diddy, Kamala Harris, and the list goes on. The WNBA dedicated its entire season to Breonna and put her name on their shirts, shoes, and even the banners on the

[6] Emma Nolan, "Conservatives Point Out Oprah's Net Worth After She Attacks 'White Privilege,'" *Newsweek*, August 5, 2020, https://www.newsweek.com/oprah-winfrey-white-privilege-oprah-conversation-twitter-conservatives-1522923.

[7] David Williams, "Oprah's O Magazine puts up billboards all over Louisville demanding action in the Breonna Taylor case" *CNN,* August 19, 2020, https://www.cnn.com/2020/08/07/us/oprah-breonna-taylor-billboards-trnd/index.html

court. I'll reiterate, *I have no issue with someone re-membering her name from this tragedy, but the entire truth should be shared with that story.*

The NBA players weren't going to be out-done by the WNBA. LeBron led the charge, giving statements about an event that he only knew about from what he had heard. LeBron reportedly gets paid $300,000 per sponsored Instagram post, but you can't put a price tag on the impact of the false narrative he was spin-ning. He has a following of eighty-two million for which he was gracious enough to post his flawed and misguided opinion. He repeated-ly said he wanted us arrested and that justice needed to be served. His post shows him wearing a red MAGA hat that had been altered to read "Make America arrest the cops who killed Breonna Taylor." He was also wearing a shirt that said "By Any Means." This proc-lamation comes from a guy who thinks pretty highly of himself. He wears a shirt that says James 3:16 and has a tattoo across his back that says "THE CHOSEN 1." This is another oppressed billionaire who is 6'9" and 250 lbs. of muscle and claims he's scared to walk down the street because he may get gunned down by police. With that large of a following, many of them being young black males, it's reckless to paint that picture of the police. It simply is not true and causes division.

WNBA dedicates season to Breonna Taylor and Say Her Name campaign

By Leah Asmelash, CNN

Updated 4:40 PM EDT, Sat July 25, 2020

(CNN) — Before the start of its 2020 campaign on Saturday, the WNBA dedicated the season to Breonna Taylor and the Say Her Name movement, which raises awareness for Black female victims of police violence.

The New York Liberty and the Seattle Storm held a 26-second long moment of silence in honor of Taylor, who was 26 years old when she was killed.

Snoop Dogg also had it all wrong in his Instagram post that garnished almost a million likes.

He said we had the wrong home, didn't knock, didn't announce, and that the person we were looking for was already in jail. Where do these celebrities get their information? And then Joe Rogan liked the tweet. Come on, Joe. I know you guys love your weed together, but that should make you know more than anyone that stoners aren't always up-to-date on their facts. Snoop was trying to drop it like it's hot, but influencing almost a million people with false information ain't cool.

Ice Cube shared countless posts with a wanted poster with our faces, names, and calling us the "MURDERERS" who killed Breonna Taylor.

Then there's the new political insider and choice of President Biden for his first interview: one of the elite minds of our day, Cardi B. There were *seventeen million views* of her ignorant stance on the case. She stated

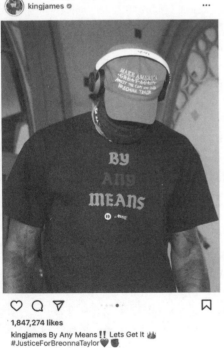

kingjames ✔   ···

1,847,274 likes
kingjames By Any Means ‼️ Lets Get It 👏
#JusticeForBreonnaTaylor 🖤 🙏
View all 22,317 comments
cassyathenaphoto 🙌🏽 🙌🏽
iamjamiefoxx Let's gooooooo!!!! 👏👏👏 🐐🐐🐐
August 18, 2020

snoopdogg ✔   ···

The Louisville Metro Police Department charged him with attempted murder because he shot in self-defense when the police raided his home, THE WRONG HOME, DIDN'T KNOCK, UNANNOUNCED, shooting 20 times, with eight of those bullets killing his girlfriend 26 year old #BreonaTaylor who was a EMT Working at 2 hospitals during the Covid -19 crisis.

Kenneth has NO criminal history for drugs or violence, and is licensed to carry. To make matters worse the suspect they were actually looking for was already in jail 👀 👀 #FreeKennethWalker #JusticeForBreona Taylor.

BLACK LIVES MATTER ‼️

Liked by joerogan and 929,116 others
snoopdogg 🍃 🙏 👊🏾
View all 19,283 comments
June 5

we ransacked Breonna's home then murdered her. That sounds more like a home-invasion robbery that ended in murder. That is nothing like what took place.

Then there was one of Louisville's most well-known actresses and someone I had cheered for, Jennifer Lawrence, jumping on the murder bandwagon of white guilt. She posted a letter on her Twitter page demanding that Attorney General Daniel Cameron bring immediate action against the officers involved. The last line of the letter said, "We must not allow the erasure of Black women to continue in America."

Then there was the Queen B of the female music world, Beyoncé. In her lengthy letter to Attorney General Cameron, she referred to justice yet said Cameron should take swift and decisive action by arresting

Ice Cube @
@icecube

WANTED:

The three MURDERERS who killed Breonna Taylor!

Sgt. Jonathan Mattingly   Brett Hankison   Myles Cosgrove

5:52 PM · 6/18/20 · Twitter for iPad

66.5K Retweets 109K Likes

11:18

IAMCARDIB
Posts   Follow

iamcardib @

2:25 Remaining

On March 13, 2020, Breonna Taylor was fatally shot by Louisville Metro Police Department (LMPD) officers.

🍿 Keep Watching

17,094,934 views

iamcardib BREONNATAYLOR · Let me tell ya something.This is why we gotta keep fighting .Breonna Taylor was one year younger then me .Pose ,dress, live her life how we do !Imagine if this happens to YOUR FRIEND ,YOUR SISTER.This is her mother telling you her story .They tried to trick her mom that night into believing maybe a enemy killed her when in fact The police ransacked her home and murdered her .They tried to sweep the case under the rug specially since the country when on lockdown due to Coronavirus.DONT LET KENTUCKY POLICE DEPARTMENT GET AWAY WITH THIS SHIT!!!!They always pull out criminal records to taint every black men or women that gets murdered by police or an excuse why they got killed .Well what's the excuse now ?! John Mattingly,Brett Hankison,Myles Cosgrove. YA NEED TO GO TO JAIL !!! THAT Wayyy ....I'll leave a link on my story FOR YOU TO HELP! #doyouknowbreonnataylorstory #sayhername

View all 17,419 comments

sweetcain50 @cubayenys they sure do I'm over here in Canada 🇨🇦 we should I can meet and talk to her she's so smart

Jennifer Lawrence - Represent.Us ✓ 🐦
@JLawrence_RepUs

#SayHerName #BreonnaTaylor

For three months since her murder, Breonna Taylor's family, the people of Louisville, Americans across the country, and many around the world have called out for justice. And yet, those calls have gone unanswered. No arrests have been made, the officers responsible for her death remain employed by the LMPD, and disturbingly, the LMPD's own investigation report was woefully inaccurate. As a Louisvillian, as a human being, I cannot be silent.

I join all those who are speaking out against this grave injustice, calling upon Attorney General Daniel Cameron to take immediate action to hold those responsible for her death accountable. Mr. Cameron, the longer you wait to bring criminal charges against officers Jonathan Mattingly, Myles Cosgrove, and Brett Hankison, the more trust erodes. I urge you to commit to transparency in the investigation and prosecution of these officers, and address the LMPD's insufficient response to Breonna Taylor's murder. We must not allow the erasure of Black women to continue in America.

As many activists and leaders have been imploring for years:
#SayHerName

♡ 8,046   4:38 PM - Jun 17, 2020   ⓘ

💬 3,807 people are talking about this   ⟩

the officers involved. Justice is supposed to be blind. Justice should take place once the investigation is completed in an unbiased manner. But justice to simple-minded people who don't know the real facts is only measured by the outcome they desire.

June 14, 2020

The Honorable Daniel Cameron
Office of the Attorney General
700 Capital Avenue, Suite 118
Frankfort, Kentucky 40601

Dear Attorney General Cameron:

It has now been over three months since members of the Louisville Metro Police Department (LMPD) killed Breonna Taylor. Plainclothes officers with a "no-knock" warrant forced their way into her apartment, where she was asleep and unarmed. Moments later, the officers fired over twenty shots into Breonna Taylor's home, striking her at least eight times. While "Breonna's Law" passed in Louisville and federal legislation has been introduced that will also ban no-knock warrants, these small steps in the right direction are painful reminders that there has still been no justice for Breonna Taylor or her family.

Three months have passed -- and the LMPD's investigations have created more questions than answers. Their incident report states that Ms. Taylor suffered no injuries – yet we know she was shot at least eight times. The LMPD officers claim they announced themselves before forcing their way into Ms. Taylor's apartment – but her boyfriend who was with her, as well as several neighbors, all say that this is untrue.

Three months have passed -- and zero arrests have been made, and no officers have been fired. The LMPD's investigation was turned over to your office, and yet all of the officers involved in the shooting remain employed by the LMPD. Sgt. Jonathan Mattingly and Officers Myles Cosgrove and Brett Hankison must be held accountable for their actions.

Three months have passed -- and Breonna Taylor's family still waits for justice. Ms. Taylor's family has not been able to take time to process and grieve. Instead, they have been working tirelessly to rally the support of friends, their community, and the country to obtain justice for Breonna.

Your office has both the power and the responsibility to bring justice to Breonna Taylor, and demonstrate the value of a Black woman's life. I urge you to use that power and:

1. Bring criminal charges against Jonathan Mattingly, Myles Cosgrove, and Brett Hankison.

2. Commit to transparency in the investigation and prosecution of these officers' criminal conduct.

3. Investigate the LMPD's response to Breonna Taylor's murder, as well the pervasive practices that result in the repeated deaths of unarmed Black citizens.

Don't let this case fall into the pattern of no action after a terrible tragedy. With every death of a Black person at the hands of the police, there are two real tragedies: the death itself, and the inaction and delays that follow it. This is your chance to end that pattern. Take swift and decisive action in charging the officers. The next months cannot look like the last three.

Sincerely,

Beyoncé Knowles-Carter

Suddenly, I couldn't turn on the radio or TV, log on to social media, or even read the paper without someone saying her name and disparaging me and those involved that evening. I have records of hundreds of movie stars, athletes, performers, news stations, television shows, documentaries, and magazines that used their platforms to defame and slander us officers involved. We've been framed to be murderers by almost every single one of them. We've been called racist and the KKK. They have said we were at the wrong apartment and killed her while she was asleep in her bed during a botched raid. These lies have never been corrected by these so-called social justice warriors, causing tens if not hundreds of millions of people to buy into these lies. I was attacked on Facebook, Twitter, and LinkedIn with death threats due to these false posts.

A GoFundMe was set up for Tamika Palmer. Celebrities were showing support by donating money, and the exposure given to the page helped it raise $6,815,190 as of the writing of this book. I don't begrudge anyone wanting to give their hard-earned money to any cause or person they want. I know the family was in pain, and people were showing their support. I do however have an issue with some of the wording about the cause that the donations were going to support: "Fire and revoke the pensions of the officers that murdered Breonna. Arrest, charge, and convict them for the murder of Breonna Taylor." If you gave to this fund, you supported this cause.

There's one other looming issue that I'll get back to later: the murder-for-hire implications against us officers. That raised concern for us families on the other side of this tragedy. Kenneth Walker—you know, the guy who shot a cop—also set up a GoFundMe page and raised over $220,000 for his defense fund. The only problem was that the charges were dropped.

A friend begged me to allow them to set up my own GoFundMe. I was against it. I hated asking for help and certainly didn't want to ask for money. I had lost a lot of money due to this incident, but God had been good to me. This friend convinced me to allow them to go forward with it, so I caved. They set up the GoFundMe, and it took off quickly. There was nothing offensive or against the rules and standards, but the page had been up for seven hours before it was suddenly pulled down by GoFundMe. They said it violated their policies and refunded the money to the donors. The person who set it up asked for an explanation as to what was violated. They refused to answer and simply sent a copy of their policies. We thoroughly read through the policies and there was no violation.

GoFundMe refused to allow the page yet allowed the guy who shot me to raise $220,000 on his first page. An additional page was set up later where another $110,000 was donated to Kenneth Walker. The bias against police and the immense pressure put on by these celebrities even extended to crowd funding organizations. The low blows just seemed to keep coming. I've asked myself on many occasions, "Do the good guys ever win?"

There was a beacon of light in the midst of this smear campaign. I had never personally met or talked to this guy at this point, but all of the sudden I actually had a black man with a large following supporting and defending me: Brandon Tatum. The Lord knew I needed someone in my corner, and He provided it to me through Brandon. A former police officer in Arizona and now a conservative influencer, he runs Tatumreport.com and speaks on conservative issues from a black man's point of view.

The GoFundMe Team (GoFundMe)
To: United We Stand
Thu 9/24/2020 8:37 PM

Dear GoFundMe Customer,

We are writing to inform you that your GoFundMe has been removed due to a violation of our Terms of Service.

The content of your fundraiser falls under our "Conditions of Use" section. You can view our Terms of Service by clicking this link.

Unfortunately, our Terms of Service, along with strictly enforced policies from the payments industry, prohibit GoFundMe from allowing you to continue raising money for this campaign. Any donations made to your fundraiser that have not already been withdrawn have been refunded and will be returned to your donors within 3-7 business days.

Regards,

The GoFundMe Team

Brandon would take his YouTube shows to lay out the leaked reports and go into detail picking them apart. If there was something he disagreed with, he spoke on it as well. His criticism wasn't one-sided, so it gave his point of view more credibility. As a bonus, it was fact-filled and not emotion-driven. He was brave for sticking his neck out and speaking the truth on what he believes regardless of the hate he received. Brandon ran his own campaign to raise money for our family and his followers blew us away. If you gave to my family or supported Tatum during this period, my family wants to thank you! God used you.[8]

The support was encouraging, but the next several months would feel like I was walking uphill in mud up to my waist while carrying heavy weights on my shoulders.

---

[8] To watch my interview with Brandon Tatum, please see "Meet Sgt. Mattingly—The Truth about Breonna Taylor," YouTube, August 24, 2021, **https://www.youtube.com/watch?v=yNYCIFenvh8.**

CHAPTER 9

ON AN ISLAND

The summer and fall of 2020 was filled with a roller coaster of emotions. After a few weeks of my entire family being in seclusion, my older children and siblings had to return to work. The world doesn't stop for any one tragedy, but our world had certainly been turned upside down. This was anything but "returning to normal" for my family. I requested that the department abandon security on me and use those resources for my children. I would be too far to assist them if something were to happen. Being of no use is a father's worst fear. I'd always been the protector, and now I had to trust in others to play my role.

Due to the doxing, any location thought to be associated with me had been put out on social media for the wolves to come knocking, and that they did. Sam Aguiar, the local attorney for Breonna Taylor's family, played right along in this evil game. He released the lawsuits to the public without the addresses being redacted, when he must have known the mob mentality in the city that he had helped perpetuate with outlandish, theatrical allegations. Caravans began to form with hundreds of angry individuals. These groups would use Facebook to post meeting locations and their intentions to get justice. We sold our house in January of 2020 to a couple from India. The day the mob decided this was still my residence, they surrounded the house and were chanting and screaming. The police responded and explained to these fools that we no longer lived there and hadn't for months. The poor new homeowner and her three kids were escorted from the house terrified and in tears. That family moved out and sold the house.

My ex-wife's house was the next location on the hit list of this angry mob determined to do their part in getting justice. The great mob investigators came to the conclusion that the person I hadn't been married to since 2003 was suddenly my wife again. This just shows the level of ignorance of people who have been so enraged to a boiling point with a false narrative that they are willing to accept anything told to them. Then there's our friend, who happens to be a minority, who had so graciously opened her home to us and allowed us to stay while we were in transition. Her address had now been published, and a group gathered to bring the visceral hate her way. This plan was intercepted online, and the police thwarted their mission. Security was placed at these residences due to the volatility that still persisted in the city.

The protests continued on a daily basis. Clashes with police continued, and city leaders continued to cower. By this time, the officers involved felt like we had been abandoned and were left on an island to fend for ourselves. Our original defense lawyer represented all three officers in the case. Looking back, that was a mistake, but neither myself nor our FOP had been through anything like this, so I just went with whom the FOP sent. Lesson learned. The attorney is a good man and has successfully defended many a police officer. Once the case was sent to the attorney general's office, our attorney was instructed he must recuse himself and not defend any of us. The reason given was that we could all receive different charges stemming from the events that night, and the attorney would have conflicts since he represented all of us. Now months into this debacle, we were left with no legal representation.

I began to reach out to some of the best defense attorneys in Louisville. I knew the narrative being spun, and regardless of my innocence, I needed a good attorney. As I went down the list of respected attorneys, the picture started coming into focus. We were untouchable and not in a good way. Good defense attorneys are good because of the clientele they represent. Naturally there are innocent people that come through the court system that deserve justice, but prisons aren't full of innocent people. The good attorneys are the ones who can find legal loopholes, can argue there is reasonable doubt, or are simply great at theatrics and lying. I called eight of these lawyers. Not one single lawyer would touch any of us with a ten-foot pole. Only one lawyer out of the group had the guts to tell me what I already knew. He told me that, due to his clientele base, taking me on would destroy his business. While disappointed, I gained respect for this man on that day. No one wanted to be canceled, and from a logical

standpoint I can't say I blame them. It did start to open my eyes to things. Suddenly, the privileges afforded some were not being afforded to others due to race and profession. So, I guess Oprah was wrong. My whiteness didn't give me that unfair advantage or even a fair playing field. I'm simply a white guy in a WOKE world.

I must admit, some of the propaganda was creative. I wonder what some of the people who spend their time harassing others could do if they redirected their energy.

Others overtly posted threats like this pact signed in blood to avenge her death:

It is done 🔪🔪🔪 ... \ ⁄⁄✕🔴 Breonna Taylor will be avenged

About three weeks after we had relocated to the safe house, my five-year-old and I were out exploring around our street and playing with his Nerf guns. We were in a pretty secluded area, and cars seldom came down this road. A maroon Nissan Altima with tinted windows crept slowly by the house and stopped right in front of it. My mind instantly went to the worst possible scenario. We were off the road, and the car didn't initially see us. I told my son to wait where he was, and I approached the vehicle. As I got up to the driver's side of the car, it sped off. My police instincts kicked in. I ran inside with my son and grabbed my keys. I jumped in my car and rode around looking for this vehicle. Little did I know, while I was gone, my son told my wife that he would protect her if anybody came, and he watched out the window the entire time. Learning that information tore my heart out. No five-year-old should have to worry that someone is coming to get him or his family. My wife was a nervous wreck, but I hadn't felt my senses this heightened since March 13. I located what I thought was the vehicle and sent a picture of the tag to Kevin, who ran the tag and immediately reached back out to us. The car was registered to someone with the last name of Walker. Since Kenneth Walker was the person who shot me, my wife went into panic mode. A little deeper research showed there was no correlation between the two—this time, things were just a coincidence, and there was no threat.

There were many occasions where my son told my wife that he would protect her if the bad man came. He even told me that, if someone came for us, he was willing to die to defend us. The fact that my small son even had to think in this realm is heartbreaking and unacceptable.

One day we were hanging out with some friends, and my phone rang. A law enforcement officer told me that the ATF had called several agents in to assist with a motorcycle gang out of Chicago that was reportedly headed to Louisville to meet up with the clubs involved in the hit placed on us. When the threats first began, we were told that the original plan was to contract this nationwide club and the chapter out of Chicago, and they would be the group to carry out the hit. This wasn't far-fetched. This club did come to Louisville to support its sister clubs after Taylor's death, and we do have a smaller chapter in Louisville. I was told that ATF had received word that some hit was taking place that weekend, and they were monitoring the group from Chicago. We were given descriptions of three different cars and two accompanying motorcycles to look out for. I have no idea where this information originated or how credible it was, but the source that called had been spot-on to this point. *Here we go again*, I thought. I had to call all my adult children and siblings and fill them in. Each time I called them was difficult. I felt secure but felt they were on their own even though they still had security. The weekend passed, and that threat seemed to fade away, although each traumatizing moment and threat is like a scar.

On May 31, 2020, I was told the FBI corroborated two separate threats from different sources. We received a call at 10 p.m. asking us to pack our bags and leave our house. We had to sell our house that we lived in for six weeks and have been in "hiding" ever since. The FBI opened the case and closed it after just two and a half weeks, from all the intel I can gather. I had secret clearance with the FBI, and that process took about a year to get. I obtained it because some of the detectives I supervised were task force officers with the FBI. I have NEVER seen a case, on a federal level, opened and closed that quickly. I've seen cases left open for months and years because it's easier to leave the case open than to shut it and try and open a new one. "Optics" was the buzzword when talking of going after a mother in a nationally sensitive case. It didn't matter that she allegedly knew about a hit out on cops. The higher-ups at the FBI deemed the informant unreliable as a way to close the case. The informant in fact was not unreliable and was still active on a separate case that's an active OCDETF (Organized Crime Drug Enforcement Task Force) case with the ATF. Once the Feds deem an informant unreliable, no one can use them for federal cases. A source close to the case asked one of the FBI bosses what we were supposed to do since they refused to investigate the case. His response: tell them to relocate.

Stay with me. Here's where it gets good. The Louisville Metro Chief of Public Safety is Amy Hess. Chief Hess came to work in Louisville in December of 2019, leaving the FBI as the highest ranking female official ever in the FBI. She worked in DC and was appointed by James Comey. From what I've been told by a source that used to work for her, she's allegedly a BLM sympathizer and liberal (like our mayor). I don't know if that's true, but I do know this mayor puts only those of like mind around him. She's very close friends with the Special Agent in Charge in the Louisville field office of the FBI. She allegedly talks to him daily on the phone, per a source that knows them both. One of Hess's key words frequently used is *optics*, which was the original "bad optics" consensus of the FBI bosses. From day one Mayor Fischer pandered to the black community and Breonna Taylor's family, as did Governor Andy Beshear. Fischer and Beshear continuously said we needed justice for Breonna and to keep her legacy alive, and they promoted "peaceful" protesting. Fischer never once mentioned me, the physical trauma, or the threats, nor did he refute the false information. He allowed the lawyers to create and guide the narrative in the case from the beginning without correcting any of it. We had a gag order on us from the courts, but they had freedom to say anything they wanted. Everything was a lie.

I'm not saying this happened, because I have no hard evidence, but due to the circumstantial evidence, it's my belief and my theory alone, that Amy Hess called her buddy and asked him to close the case on the murder-for-hire. I'm sure it was spun that it would look bad for any future promotions if he stuck his neck out and actually did the right thing, or maybe it was just a friend calling in a favor for her boss. When I ran this theory by David James during a phone call, he said that would make sense. He went on to say that ever since she was hired by the mayor, the information from the explorer case (another case the mayor and chief tried to keep from the public) had been difficult to get from the FBI. Who knows? I do know the agents running the case were outraged that they were forced to close it, and all they were told is that those above them had closed the case. Mind you, they (the people who made the decision) had never talked to the informant themselves but still labeled that person unreliable.

On a side note, the Louisville Special Agent in Charge at the time of this questionable closing of the investigation has been given a promotion and is now in Washington, DC. Coincidence? Maybe, but there's been an awful lot of coincidences in this case that did not favor those of us involved in this incident. Amy Hess no longer works for the city. She mysteriously stepped down after I gave a recorded statement to the department on my theory of her involvement with the FBI case. Maybe that had nothing to do with her decision, but it was awfully convenient timing. Several of our upper command were shown the door along with our civilian public information director who marched with the protesters and was rumored to have been sharing information with leaders of these protests.

The optics would look bad on Fischer if the family he backed was found to have known about a hit placed on the cops. They received almost $7 million from GoFundMe and $12 million in the lawsuit. I have no idea if that money led to action. Maybe it was just talk out of anger and hurt. Maybe there was validity to it. We will never know because a politically driven machine chooses optics over lives.

No agency is looking at them or gathering intel, which leaves our families in limbo and constantly looking over our shoulders. The FBI refused to talk with me. I've requested a meeting through my chain of command, but I was told it would be a conflict of interest even though the investigations were being run through two different divisions and I was the victim in this particular case. Breonna Taylor's family has been afforded the opportunity to meet with them about the case being investigated for civil rights violations against the officers involved. The FBI even met with Christopher 2X, a local activist. Heck, even a group of teenagers for social justice were afforded a meeting with the FBI to give their opinion on the case. My attorney called, yet as a victim I was refused contact and information on the case involving me as the target of the threat. It took my attorney a month to get a straight answer—the case was indeed closed—from the US Attorney assigned the case. This only came after we were given the runaround. Since the case was closed, I requested my attorney file an FOIA (Freedom of Information Act) for the case file so we could get another agency to run with the case. The FOIA was received by Washington, DC, and we got an email back saying the request would receive expedited treatment due to the merits of the case.

We never received any information or documents. My attorney filed another FOIA and spoke with a representative of the DOJ who assured him she'd walk the paperwork through and expedite the information requested. Again, we heard nothing. It's now been over ten months since we moved out of our house due to these threats, and the FBI has still never talked to me one time about this case. My attorneys reached out yet again and were told, due to the fact that there were never any charges placed, they would not release the case file. They would not give any explanation as to why there were no charges, did not reassure us there were no threats, and would not go on record as to why the case was closed. These are what we call red flags. Lack of transparency has been the common theme through this entire ordeal even though people on both sides have begged for it. Everyone wants and deserves the truth. Mayor Fischer pounds his chest about being transparent, yet he is the most soiled of the bunch when it comes to transparency. It only applies when it's in his favor. When transparency is not given, all trust is lost.

I reached out and talked to higher-up representatives of both Sen. McConnell and Sen. Rand Paul. I explained my frustrations, the dilemma with the FBI, and my theories based on those dilemmas. McConnell's office said that, while they understand my frustration and feel sorry for us, they can't get involved with an FBI investigation. The talk with Rand Paul's

U.S. Department of Justice

Executive Office for United States Attorneys

Freedom of Information and Privacy Staff | Suite 5-400, 5CON Building | (202) 252-6020
175 N Street, NE | FAX (202) 252-6048
Washington, DC 20530

July 16, 2020

Kent Wicker
Dressman Benzinger Lavelle PSC
2100 Waterfront Plaza
321 West Main Street
Louisville, KY 40202
kwicker@dblaw.com

Re: Request Number: EOUSA-2020-003494
Date of Receipt: July 16, 2020
Subject of Request: Criminal Investigation Records Regarding a Murder for Hire Against John
                   Mattingly or Myles Cosgrove/ USAO- Eastern District of Kentucky

Dear Mr. Wicker:

        This is in response to your recent letter requesting expedited treatment of your pending
Freedom of Information Act/Privacy Act request.

        After careful consideration of your letter, I have decided that your Freedom of
Information Act/Privacy Act request merits expedited treatment by this office. Therefore, your
request will be pulled out of chronological order and appropriate actions to process your request
will begin.

        The above action by this office does not imply that you will receive a response within the
statutory time limits. You will, however, receive a response to your Freedom of Information
Act/Privacy Act request as soon as possible.

                                        Sincerely,

                                        Kevin Krebs
                                        Assistant Director

Form No. 014 – 4/11

people seemed to go well. They asked if I would be willing to come in and meet with some other individuals in his office to discuss my concerns. Heck yes, I was willing. I was told to await a call back and the meeting would get set up. I was optimistic, but that's as far as that went. I never heard back. I didn't waste my breath with Representative John Yarmuth. He had already made his stance known, and he had clearly planted his flag on the other side of the aisle. Maybe I'll run for his seat in congress in 2022.

At this point I had run out of options. My chief had no contact with me. My mayor had chosen his side. The city council president wasn't willing to take a stand in public and say anything in our favor. The governor made his position clear that he thought we were in the wrong. My two senators blew me off, and my Congressman, John Yarmuth, had already taken a hard stance against us. Then on March 11, 2021, Yarmuth gave a floor speech in the House of Representatives slamming the police. *"There's no mystery about the killers' identities. And yet, they remain free.*

"That this is unjust, tragic, an abomination should be beyond debate. Instead, it is hardly unique in America for two reasons: Because the killers wore badges, and their victims were Black."[9]

Where could I go from there? It was like those of us involved had leprosy. It was an election year, and this case had become a political talking point. People of influence were scared to do the right thing and take a stand in this case.

Late June, right in the middle of our threats, the NASCAR and Bubba Wallace hate crime story made national news. Wallace found what he believed to be a noose hanging in his garage at Talladega Superspeedway. The FBI made it a priority to send fifteen agents to the speedway to investigate this dangerous rope, but it was determined that the "noose" was actually a garage door rope pull that had been in this garage since 2019 and had absolutely nothing to do with Bubba Wallace or the fact he's a black man. The evil rope was actually tied with a loop for functionality to make it easier to hold on to while pulling the garage door closed.

I have no issue with the FBI investigating to see if an overt threat had been placed on Bubba Wallace. I think it's their duty. Fifteen agents, however, was a bit of overkill and possibly a PR move on their part. The thing that infuriates me is the willingness to put that many resources to investigate an inanimate object, but to refuse to investigate actual death threats on police officers due to "optics."

There are too many coincidences that point to corruption. Who investigates the FBI and our politicians? Who holds them accountable? I will not be silent, and I will continue to fight. We were used as pawns in the mayor and city council's political careers. In the meantime, that game is destroying or at least forever altering people's lives. It has taken the career I loved away from me. It has turned a city that I loved and served against me.

In a strange turn of events, the City of Louisville passed a law banning no-knock warrants. The name of the law is Breonna's Law. This name has

9 https://www.wlky.com/amp/article/kentucky-rep-yarmuth-honors-breonna-taylor-on-house-floor-says-her-killers-remain-free/35812779

spread like wildfire throughout the nation, attaching it to the banning or restrictions of no-knock warrants. The irony is that the warrant that led to Breonna's death wasn't executed as a no-knock. I still believe in my heart that, had we served the warrant as a no-knock, Breonna would be alive, and you would not be reading this book.

Mayor Fischer's speech during the signing ceremony was the same rhetoric he had been spewing all along. "Thank you to those whose emphatic cries of enough have fueled the marches, the protests, the movement sweeping our country, sweeping our city and have filled the streets of America and helped bring us to this moment," Fischer said. "This of course, is just one step, one victory forward in the fight for justice and peace and equity in our city and nation."[10]

Governor Beshear signed a similar bill into Kentucky law later. His statements, while possibly well intended, were hollow and just a political speech. "I am signing Senate Bill 4 to help ensure no other mother knows Tamika Palmer's grief at the loss of her daughter Breonna Taylor," Beshear said. "This is meaningful change and will save lives."[11] I also hope no mother feels the grief of Tamika Palmer. However, signing a law that didn't pertain to the events of that night but that further muddies the water of what really took place will do nothing to curb criminal activity that leads the police to individuals' doors in the first place.

The most excruciating part during these months was the time away from my older kids and grandkid. While they had 24-hour security, there were events that arose that brought sheer terror to me. One occasion was a vehicle that stopped in front of my daughter's house and took photos. The occupants were followed to a parking lot where they discarded three bags of trash. The trash was collected for evidence. There was trash from three different locations, which was run through our databases. One of the addresses had previously been rented by a different John/Jonathan Mattingly. The male passenger was identified as a Salvadorian male. I knew that the MS-13 gang is a violent gang with deep roots from Salvador, so my hyper-vigilant mindset put me on edge. There are no coincidences

[10] "Mayor Fischer signs 'Breonna's Law' banning no-knock warrants in Louisville," WDRB.com, June 12, 2020, https://www.wdrb.com/news/mayor-fischer-signs-breonnas-law-banning-no-knock-warrants-in-louisville/article_0c3b5110-acd7-11ea-9346-c7fa0eb55532.html.

[11] Rachel Treisman, "Kentucky Law Limits Use of No-Knock Warrants, a Year After Breonna Taylor's Killings," NPR, April 9, 2021, https://www.npr.org/2021/04/09/985804591/kentucky-law-limits-use-of-no-knock-warrants-a-year-after-breonna-taylors-killin.

in police work. That a vehicle pulled in front of my daughter's house and took a picture while having trash in their vehicle that belonged to a residence where a John Mattingly lived sent chills down my spine. Another incident occurred where a black male circled the block a few times and was found in his vehicle parked across the street from my daughter's house. He was identified and a background check was completed, which found that he was an associate of one of the motorcycle clubs that had reportedly taken the hit out on the families.

Below is the text taken from two emails that I sent on July 20 and 23 to then-acting Chief Robert Schroeder and the chain of command involved in the protection detail:

On Sunday July 19

A 2010 blue Ford Escape KY tags ****** slow rolled past the front of the residence. The vehicle then circled the block and parked across the street from the residence. I did not receive how long the vehicle was parked there nor was I informed of the description of the subject. The vehicle came back to 103 ***** Ave * Louisville, KY.

  - I'm not sure who this information was passed on to or when, however, when I spoke with Officer *****, who was assigned the detail the following day, he knew nothing about this incident or vehicle description.

  - As far as I was told neither CIC nor RTTC was notified of the vehicle or tag. No complete background was completed on the vehicle, the address the vehicle is registered to, nor the subjects' acquaintances etc.

  - The vehicle was not followed from the location to see its final destination.

On Monday July 20th approximately 2140

  A 2001 Chevy Impala (unknown color) KY tags ****** pulled in front of the same residence. The vehicle was occupied by a female driver and male passenger. The female passenger rolled down her window and took photos of the house and vehicles. As the vehicle pulled off, the officer could see the female looking at the photos she had just taken. The vehicle drove to ****** apartments located at 813 **** Blvd. The male exited the vehicle and took 3 bags of trash out of the vehicle and threw them in a dumpster. The vehicle then headed toward Interstate 65 and the officer felt it was important to go back to the residence instead of following the car as this could be a diversion technique.

I notified ****** and he had not been informed of either vehicle at this point. I know ****** was going to call ****** once the information from tonight was gathered.

Around 2300 hrs I was notified that the security detail had cleared the residence at 2200 and there was no one watching the residence. I called ******* and expressed my disbelief and how dumbfounded I was that after 2 nights of suspicious activity and only 20 minutes after someone took pictures of the residence, that the officers felt it was okay to secure for the night without contacting a supervisor.

Several areas of basic investigative police work failed to be adhered to during the course of 24 hrs. 1. The initial vehicle on 7-19-2020 was disregarded as an anomaly. There are no coincidences or anomalies in this type of police work. 2. There was no extensive background, that I know of, performed on the vehicle, subject, or address. 3. The information received on 7-19-2020 was not passed on to the other crews working the security detail. That in and of itself is an officer safety issue. 4. None of the occupants in either vehicle was positively identified. This could have taken place by calling a marked car from ****** to perform a stop on the vehicle, or the cars could have been followed to Louisville and been stopped for identification. 5. The house was left unattended, and the officers secured for the evening immediately after a second incident occurred.

If the threat is significant enough to require security, then the follow-through of the officers on this detail is of the utmost importance. I'm extremely grateful for the detail and to these officers, but for the safety of ALL involved, I believe a hyper vigilance should remain when incidents out of the ordinary take place. Communication is VITAL. Sharing details whether they think are important or not, and NOT leaving a post until given the okay.

Again, THANK YOU for allowing a detail to assist us in these trying times, it does not go unappreciated. We all know the details of the murder for hire put out on us by ********. We also know the FBI closed the case and refuses contact with me as a victim. There is currently no one investigating this case even though the FBI says the threats are still credible and they advised LMPD to keep security on us. This is unacceptable and I refuse to back down. My number 1 priority is to protect my family just as yours is. I will do it at any cost and with everything in my power to do that, but I'm also asking for assistance from the department that I've given 20 years of service to and almost died in the process.

I've been victimized several times during this case, and I refuse to be a victim any longer. No one from command besides Major Burbrink reached out to me after they dismissed the charges on Kenneth Walker. No one in command had the courage to stand up and say that the civil and criminal attorneys were spreading vicious outright lies. No one from command, the department, or even the FBI reached out to tell me the FBI closed the case several weeks ago and no one IS monitoring the bank accounts or threats. I've been on an island. A little consideration and respect would be nice and the right thing to do. What happened on March 13, 2020 was a tragedy that no one wanted or anticipated. I feel for the family's loss, however, I feel more consideration has been given to Breonna Taylor's family due to fear of public opinion (which is based on false information) and the "optics" of supporting our own LMPD family, and that's fine if you can do that and look at yourself in the mirror the next day. We all answer to God for what we do or don't do.

Respectfully,
John Mattingly

Second Email:

On Thursday July 23, 2020, I received a call from an analyst from LMPD reporting back on the information that was recovered from the trash bags that the suspects from Monday night threw in a dumpster. One of the receipts in the trash had an address, that when ran through *Accurint,* comes back to a previous tenant named John/Jonathan Mattingly. This is concerning because it appears the suspects that drove to my daughter's house and took photos of her house and vehicles were also at other locations that they thought may be associated to a John Mattingly.

A little later in the day I received an additional call from a detective assisting me on the case. The owner of the vehicle from Sunday night was identified as a "hang around" from the No Haterz Motorcycle Club. This is the same club that Breonna Taylor's mother, Tamika Palmer, is a member of. This is also the same club that allegedly began circulating the fact that there is a $50,000 hit on the officers involved.

It's no coincidence that 2 vehicles on consecutive nights, have ties to No Haterz, or info that appears to be linked back to trying to figure out locations of officers. This is concerning to myself and my family since the FBI closed the case. I'm asking for you to reach out to the ATF and let them run this case. I have FBI undercover agents willing to assist but allow the ATF to fully run the case. The ATF agent that has the CI into the club is willing to get on board but needs approval from the AUSA and the agent's bosses.

This is not the time for egos to be involved. I need assistance from LMPD, ATF, AUSA. If you are unwilling, then please let me know and I will figure out alternate routes. This is not a time for complacency.

These emails fell on deaf ears once again. The silence from LMPD was more deafening than any conversation we could have at this point.

CHAPTER 10

THE WAIT

Months had gone by at this point. The protests in the city continued. Looting and destruction of property had subsided, but protesters still took over the streets and intersections at night. This was more of a nightly, unruly party than a protest, unless the police tried breaking up the disorderly party, and then all bets were off.

A small park located on the corner of 6th and Jefferson streets downtown, Jefferson Square Park, had been taken over for months by protesters. The protesters and media now called it "Injustice Square" as it was the rallying point for the protests for the past year. The park sits across the street from the courthouse on one side, the grand jury and Commonwealth Attorney's office on another side, City Hall directly across from it, and LMPD headquarters catty-corner from it. It is the epicenter of downtown Louisville and was home to both the police and firefighter's memorials who had died in the line of duty. Those memorials have since been removed due to vandalism.

This one-time beautiful, small sitting area in downtown Louisville was now covered in tents, a memorial to Breonna Taylor, and trash. Vendor tables were set up daily to sell merchandise related to Taylor and the police, and downtown became an unsafe place to go after dark. Cars would block intersections, and instigators would harass anyone who tried to get through their roadblocks. In several instances, people were pulled out of their cars and assaulted. Shots were fired from an AK-47 at a vehicle whose operator was scared and simply "disobeyed" the enforcer's orders to stop. Each group that protested and blocked intersections would have heavily armed security in body armor intimidating motorists. The police were infuriated that these events were taking place, but the mayor and chief's office wouldn't allow any enforcement to take place.

A several-block area around the park has been designated "Breewayy." Seventeen pole banners were approved by the city and hung on the corners with different quotes and pictures, all about racial justice. The images include David McAtee, Tyler Gerth, and Breonna Taylor. Each banner also has a quote on the back and is accompanied by the hashtag "Breewayy."

On June 27, Tyler Gerth, a local photographer and activist, was shot and killed in Jefferson Square Park, making him the ninth victim of gun violence due to these "peaceful" protests. Steven Lopez, 23, and another daily protester were arrested and charged with his murder. Lopez had been arrested on June 17 for inciting a riot, harassment, and disorderly conduct. The citation also said he was in possession of a handgun "with two full mags of ammo." Why on earth was Lopez out of jail? Why is it every time the police put themselves in danger to enforce the law our judicial system releases the criminals? These protesters were being released faster than the police could finish their paperwork. If you want to look at why crime is so high across America, just look at the repeat offenders. We are playing a dangerous game of catch and release. Tyler Gerth would be alive today were it not for a false narrative and a broken judicial system.

"I am deeply saddened by the violence that erupted in Jefferson Square Park tonight, where those who have been voicing their concerns have been gathered," Fischer said. "It is a tragedy that this area of peaceful protest is now a crime scene." "Voicing concerns" must be the new terminology for committing crimes. I'm so thankful for a mayor who cares so deeply about all of his constituents.

As time passed, everyone became restless awaiting the decision from Kentucky's attorney general. Between the constant doom and gloom of the coronavirus, job losses, and riots over the summer, time was dragging. Each day consisted of waking up, drinking coffee, and staring at my smartphone. Each day was a new adventure in what disparaging remarks could be said about the police today. I was so tired of seeing that horrible picture of myself all over the internet and news. Just a month before this incident, I told my wife that I hoped I would never be involved in anything where my picture is on the news. She asked me why, and I showed her my work photo, and she laughed. I hated that picture before, but now I really hate it.

The positive I've been able to take from this is the time I've been able to spend with my parents and youngest son. I've always been a workaholic, not because I love work, which I used to, but because when you have four kids and are living off a police officer's salary, you have to hump it some-times. I didn't mind putting in the hours for my family, but you can never get that time back. Fortunately for me I have an understanding family and a second chance.

Politicians in Louisville and across America took advantage of this trag-edy and used Breonna Taylor's name as a rallying cry for their elections. It's a sign of the times we live in when a candidate says voting for them will keep tragedies from happening. I guess personal accountability is a thing of the past. Joe Biden and Kamala Harris milked this tragedy for every bit they could, running on systemic racism claims and fire branding. So much for unifying the country.

Kamala Harris ✔ @KamalaHarris · 3d
There are two systems of justice when peaceful protesters are arrested and the police who murdered Breonna Taylor almost three months ago still roam free.

♡ 649   ↻ 9,122   ♡ 39K   ↑

On June 6, Rev. Jesse Jackson visited Louisville to stir the flames and to attach his face to the latest of tragedies that involved a person of color and a white police officer. While introducing Jackson, Mayor Greg Fischer said he understood why people were protesting the killings of black people in America by the police, including Breonna Taylor, and that people have had enough. He emphasized *ENOUGH!* as his fist hit the podium. He went on to say that he welcomed the protestors to Louisville. This after we'd had businesses destroyed, police officers injured, and people shot and severely hurt during these very protests. How, as the leader of a city, can you say you welcome people who negatively affect our downtown business and entertainment industries? How can you get behind your podium and say you are thankful for what they have done? He continued by saying:

> I'm grateful to the Rainbow Push Coalition and Rev. Jackson. We started talking with these folks about ten days ago. They could have chosen to be in a lot of cities today. For them to come to our great city I consider it a real privilege and honor. I want to thank again, as I close up, all the peaceful protesters. It is a crying shame

Congress of the United States
Washington, DC 20515

May 22, 2020

The Honorable Eric S. Dreiband
Assistant Attorney General
Civil Rights Division
U.S. Department of Justice
950 Pennsylvania Avenue NW
Washington, D.C. 20530

Dear Assistant Attorney General Dreiband:

We write to ask that the U.S. Department of Justice take immediate action on yet another shooting of an unarmed black person in the United States. Breonna Taylor was a 26-year-old EMT who worked for two hospitals in Louisville, Kentucky. On March 13, police officers with the Louisville Police Department SWAT team entered Ms. Taylor's apartment to execute a drug search warrant, and allegedly fired 20 shots into her apartment. Ms. Taylor was shot at least eight times. She was not a primary suspect, nor were there any drugs recovered from her home. The killing of Ms. Taylor is an unspeakable tragedy that requires immediate answers and accountability. Accordingly, we ask that the U.S. Department of Justice immediately launch an independent investigation into the shooting of Breonna Taylor, as well as a pattern or practice investigation into the Louisville Police Department for potential civil rights violations.

One day after Ms. Taylor's death, the Louisville Police Department announced that they were opening an internal investigation into the shooting and had placed the three involved officers on administrative leave. In the last two months, those officers have not been discharged by the department or charged by the district attorney's office. On May 20, Louisville Mayor Greg Fischer announced that the Louisville Police Department sent the investigative file to Kentucky Attorney General Daniel Cameron, and will send the file to the Federal Bureau of Investigation and the U.S. Attorney for the Western District of Kentucky.

The Louisville Police Department was accused of using excessive force before Ms. Taylor was killed. Two of the three officers involved in Ms. Taylor's death have been the subject of excessive force complaints.[1] Moreover, the Louisville Police Department SWAT team was involved in another drug raid last October where, after minimal investigation, they entered the home of a black family and held them at gunpoint.[2] The family alleges that the targets of the investigation did not live at the home, and this could easily have been discovered by police prior to their execution of the warrant. In light of the troubling parallels between these cases, we ask the Justice Department to conduct an independent investigation to determine whether the Louisville Police Department has engaged in a pattern or practice of constitutional violations.

that it was fifty-two years ago when the Carter Commission put out their report decrying and describing the condition of America in 1967 and 1968. When you read that report, that report could have been written last week. I'm grateful to the protesters because I'm hoping America finally wakes up. It is White America's responsibility; it is white Louisville's responsibility to lead this type of transformation. We're not looking for change. As you can go back after that, we're looking for transformation. The protesters can always count me to be an ally in this movement. After we get out of the passion of

Ms. Taylor was a young woman with plans for a long, fruitful life. Her mother has said that Ms. Taylor had planned to become a nurse, buy a home, and one day start a family. Instead, her life was brutally cut short by a haphazard law enforcement exercise. Ms. Taylor worked to save lives during the COVID-19 pandemic; it is time for the U.S. Department of Justice to honor hers. Accordingly, we ask that the U.S. Department of Justice immediately launch an independent investigation into whether Ms. Taylor's killing violated federal laws. We also ask the Department of Justice to conduct an independent investigation to determine whether there has been a pattern or practice of constitutional violations at the Louisville Police Department.

Sincerely,

Kamala D. Harris
United States Senator

Lucy McBath
United States Representative

Signatories

U.S. Senators
Richard Blumenthal
Cory A. Booker
Sherrod Brown
Kirsten Gillibrand
Amy Klobuchar
Edward J. Markey
Patty Murray
Bernard Sanders
Chris Van Hollen
Elizabeth Warren

U.S. Representatives

Alma S. Adams, Ph.D.
André Carson
Kathy Castor
Joaquin Castro
Yvette D. Clarke
Wm. Lacy Clay
Bonnie Watson Coleman
Mike Doyle
Marcia L. Fudge
Al Green
Alcee L. Hastings
Jahana Hayes
Henry C. "Hank" Johnson, Jr.
Hakeem Jeffries
Joseph P. Kennedy III
Ro Khanna

Barbara Lee
A. Donald McEachin
James P. McGovern
Gregory W. Meeks
Gwen S. Moore
Joe Neguse
Eleanor Holmes Norton
Alexandria Ocasio-Cortez
Mark Pocan
Ayanna Pressley
Cedric L. Richmond
Lisa Blunt Rochester
Bobby L. Rush
Bennie G. Thompson
Juan Vargas
Frederica S. Wilson

2

the protests, we gotta get to the work. We gotta do the road work. That's what Ali [boxing legend and Louisville native Muhammed Ali] would always say and that's what made him great. And part of doing the road work is signing up everybody to VOTE, and that we get people out to the voting booth. That's where meaningful change happens. We have some big elections coming up this November. And that's how we have to turn this moment of pain into a moment of justice. And that's how we build a city and a country of peace and equality. And that's how we prevent future tragedies. [12]

This was political propaganda at its finest. He knew better, but the elections were coming up, and he was using this tragedy to further his party's own agenda. He was breaking the backs of the very people that protected him on a daily basis to create a racial inequality issue with the police that didn't exist in this circumstance. He was giving credit to people who destroyed his city. It was a slap in the face to the entire downtown business and entertainment industry that had been destroyed. A big double middle finger to all the small business owners who lost their livelihoods due to his incompetence. Mayor Fischer, the buck stops at the top. You are responsible for your actions—in this case inactions and failure to respond accordingly.

Rev. Jackson then took the stage to address some of the issues he has with police. He started out talking about the lynchings of the past. He then said police must lose their sovereign immunity. That statement is partially correct. Qualified immunity—what the police have—is only a part of sovereign immunity. The big push in America right now is for police to lose that qualified immunity. The misrepresentation, coming either from ignorance or hate of police, of what qualified immunity actually entails, has led to this movement. Qualified immunity shields government officials from liability *if* their activities are within the scope of their office, in objective good faith, and don't violate a clearly established statutory or constitutional right of which a reasonable person would be aware. I've known former police officers who have lost their qualified immunity due to criminal acts. We were taught this in the police academy. They used to

---

[12] Louisville MetroTV (@lou_metrotv) Tweeted: LIVE—Mayor Fischer welcomes Rev. Jesse Jackson to Louisville https://t.co/wXuNAFIoCo https://twitter.com/lou_metrotv/status/1269356760122310656?s=20

ask us, "How do you like your car? How do you like your house? How do you like your job? Because if you violate someone's civil rights intentionally or commit a crime, you will not be backed. The person will sue you, and you will lose everything." That sticks with you as a young, impressionable officer.

The system is in place to shield government and individual officers from frivolous lawsuits. Once Pandora's Box is open, with endless and expensive lawsuits, there's no going back, and there will no longer be people willing to be police officers. I'm not sure if this is the agenda, but that will be the outcome, and crime will soar even higher than it has this previous year. Jackson went on to say that, if the police kill someone, they should lose their job, and that there's a bunch of laws that protect police from humanity. I'm not even sure what that means. It's a lot of word play to try and portray police in a bad light. I think humanity is something all humans have regardless of what imaginary world they'd like to live in. No one is immune from cancer, broken hearts, pain, COVID-19, and ultimately death. These asinine statements do nothing for uniting Americans and healing the divide between the people and the ones sworn to protect and serve.

After the attorney general's announcement that the grand jury did not indict any officers for Breonna Taylors death, the good reverend called for a boycott of all high-profile athletes who were considering attending the University of Louisville and the University of Kentucky. He asked professional athletes to persuade them not to come.

I've been a UofL fan my entire life. I would regularly attend football and basketball games with friends and family, and I'd rearrange schedules to watch games when I couldn't attend. That all changed when the basketball team marched in solidarity for justice for Breonna.

It all changed when the president of the university said, "Today, a grand jury indicted one of the officers involved in the killing of Breonna Taylor, but not on charges related to her killing. While I am pleased this police officer will be tried for the unnecessary violence he caused that night, I am disappointed that our justice system allows these atrocities to occur all too often with relatively little consequence." Dr. Bendapudi continued, "This announcement is a reminder that we must recommit to pursuing racial justice and pushing for changes in law enforcement, our legal system, public policy and our educational curricula. Change will not come easy. We acknowledge that the path of progress has seldom run smoothly, and we are more determined than ever to seek racial equity and justice."[13] The University of Louisville's law school began offering a class on systemic racism titled "Breonna Taylor's Louisville." Never mind the police, who keep these Louisville players safe at games, block roads during those events so your univers   ity can make millions, or simply support your university. As long as you can make a public statement condemning the popular theme while your secular university shoves this propaganda down your students' throats, it's justified. I love sports and hope to enjoy them again someday, but I'm a little jaded by all the unfounded attacks from teams and players this year.

Jefferson County Public Schools (the failed school system in Louisville) jumped at the opportunity and decided they'd throw their name in the hat and get on the murder bandwagon. We were safe from no one's slander.

Overview

Jefferson County Public Schools adopted a Racial Equity Policy almost two years before the murders of Breonna Taylor, George Floyd, and Ahmaud Arbery. The district took a bold step in not being satisfied with racial inequities in this district and set policy, practice, and expectations in place to make sweeping change.

Change will not happen overnight, HOWEVER...

JCPS

---

13 Matthew McGavic, "UofL President and AD Release Statements Following Indictment in Breonna Taylor Case," SI.com, September 23, 2020, https://www.si.com/college/louisville/othersports/president-and-ad-statement-breonna-taylor.

On June 25, Ben Crump, along with social justice antagonizers Until Freedom, organized a rally at Kentucky's State Capital. The opening line on Ben Crump's official website page that promoted the rally says, "The police officers who murdered Breonna Taylor . . . must be held accountable." This event featured Jada Pinkett Smith, Common, Kenny Stills (NFL), Porsha Williams, MC Lyte, and others. Alicia Keys received a shout-out from Tamika Mallory for her help with the rally. Keys, Common, Williams, and Stiles had been outspoken for months, tweeting and posting disparaging comments online and in magazines.

July 25 was a day full of tensions for Louisville. The NFAC (Not F#@*ing Around Coalition), a black militia group based out of Atlanta, descended on Louisville to demand justice for Breonna Taylor. A Three Percenters militia group decided they would attend the protest the same day to support the police and protect the city if necessary. During the assembly of the NFAC in a nearby field, one of their members had an accidental discharge of a rifle. Three of their members were struck by the gunfire and injured. The police and Louisville Fire did what they always do and ran in to assist. Fortunately for Louisville, that was the extent of the drama that day, and no one from either group caused any issues. Grandmaster Jay gave a fiery speech and warned Daniel Cameron that, if he didn't have a conclusion to the case within four weeks, they'd be back. Cameron wasn't intimidated by this group or any other outside pressure and continued his job.

On July 14, protesters descended on Daniel Cameron's new residence in Louisville. Cameron was set to get married on July 31, and this was his and

his soon-to-be bride's new home. Activist Tamika Mallory (Until Freedom) was a leader in the demonstration. Reality TV stars Porsha Williams
(*Real Housewives of Atlanta*) and Yandy Smith (*Love & Hip Hop*) were present,
and conveniently the cameras from one of the shows were rolling. Talk
about a photo op and publicity for the shows. The protesters were sitting
on the lawn while some were banging on the front door and windows.
These peaceful demonstrators were chanting that, if they didn't get what
they wanted, they would burn it down—in a peaceful kind of way and
all. They were asked several times by the police to leave and warned that,
if they didn't get off the private property, they would be arrested. These
lawful commands were ignored, and eighty-seven people were arrested
and charged with intimidating a participant in a legal process, which is a
felony, disorderly conduct, and criminal trespassing.

In a statement given by Cameron after the attempt of bullying, he said
his office planned to conduct a "thorough and fair" investigation, and
Tuesday's protests "will not alter our pursuit of the truth." He continued,
"The stated goal of today's protest at my home was to 'escalate.' That is
not acceptable and only serves to further division and tension within our
community. Justice is not achieved by trespassing on private property, and
it's not achieved through escalation. It's achieved by examining the facts

in an impartial and unbiased manner. That is exactly what we are doing and will continue to do in this investigation."[14]

In a shocking letter sent out on behalf of the County Attorney Mike O'Connell, all charges were dismissed against the individuals arrested that day. He said, "In the interest of justice and the free exchange of ideas, we will dismiss the charges for each protester this past Tuesday." So now, threatening someone and saying that you will burn their house down if you don't get your desired outcome is nothing more than a free exchange of ideas? Would Mike O'Connell agree if the families of everyone he charged showed up at *his* residence and threatened *him*? His daughter is a circuit court judge in Jefferson County. Would he appreciate it if the people she had in front of her court attempted to intimidate and threaten her? I highly doubt it.

[14] John P. Wise and Shelly Sylvestri, "AG Daniel Cameron 'Not acceptable' for protestors to stage demonstration in his yard," WAVE 3 News, July 15, 2020, https://www.wave3.com/2020/07/14/ag-daniel-cameron-not-acceptable-protesters-stage-demonstra-tion-his-yard/.

During this time period, I was sent pictures from friends still in Lou-isville who would be out somewhere and see posters in businesses, stick-ers on poles, and in White Castle drive-throughs, flyers on vehicles in Walmart parking lots, signs in our local Heine Brothers' Coffee shop, and everywhere in between. The propaganda machine was hard at work. I'm not sure who paid for all of these materials, but the message was being put out like a friend that started a multi-level marketing business. It was unavoidable.

The first week of August, I received a letter in the mail. I saw the en-velope had a return address of our police department, but the postage stamp was from Jacksonville, Florida. I knew this wasn't a get-well card, and what I discovered disgusted me: a picture of Breonna with something that resembled blood all over her face. What kind of person uses their time and resources to do this type of thing? This was more disrespectful to the memory of Breonna than to me.

Postcards were sent out to the neighborhoods and surrounding areas where we lived in an effort to intimidate us and sway our neighbors.

I can't describe the anxiety and exhaustion during this period. Being on high alert for months at a time takes a toll. Every unrecognized vehicle, every long stare in public…is it friend or foe? The strange numbers that call your phone … The rumors of the decision coming … There was no break. There was no taking it easy. I tried, but it seemed like every time I let my

guard down a new threat arose. It's been over a year, and we are still waiting on the outcome from the FBI and DOJ investigation. Too bad they couldn't wrap that up in two and a half weeks like they did the investigation into the death threats. Our faith, great friends, and family got us through.

I gave my statement to the attorney general's office on September 14, 2020. I've testified in court numerous times and given statements before, but I've never been on this side of the table. I've never given a statement that would determine the fate of my freedom. While I was a little nervous,

I knew in my heart I'd be fine. My story had never changed, and it wasn't going to on this day because it was the truth! You don't have to rehearse the truth; you just tell it. My attorneys and I met in Frankfort to be interviewed. We walked in and showed our driver's licenses and received name tags. One of the investigators on the case met us at the secured door and let us in. Two of the assistant attorney generals were sitting on the opposite side of the table waiting. We made introductions and began the interview. I'm usually pretty good at getting a read on people, but not on this day. The panel members questioning me were very professional and stoic. There was no small talk and no showing of emotion—just business, as it should have been. I believe the interview lasted a little over an hour, and we left. I felt good about the interview as I was able to answer a few questions I hadn't been asked previously and delve deeper into the details of that night.

Although I felt good about having the interview over with, I was emotionally and mentally drained. How long before they made a decision? Was I the last person they needed to interview? Was there a chance I could get charged for protecting my life? What about the guys who were just trying to protect me after I had been shot? All these thoughts ran through my head.

Little did I know that the night before my meeting with the attorney general's office, the mayor, county attorney or his representative, and the attorneys representing Breonna Taylor's family met in secrecy to agree on a $12 million settlement. The settlement also included police reform agreements. The timing of this settlement was bizarre to say the least. Why would you settle the city's largest settlement *before* hearing any of the testimony or evidence, or before any criminal charges were decided on? Red flag #1.

Not one of the attorneys slated to defend the officers as city officials was notified that a settlement had been reached. The city council was not notified either and was taken aback by the settlement, as they generally have to approve a dollar amount in a lawsuit this large. Red flag #2.

The lawsuit against us officers and the city had been amended weeks prior to the settlement. They finally took out some of the fabricated material, but the damage was done, and the narrative was set. However, it added a new twist, accusing the mayor of using his office and political influence to direct the police to clear out the entire block of Elliott Avenue as part of a gentrification project. I don't know if any of what Sam Aguiar posed in the lawsuit was true or not. I know Sam continually made false statements about the police, so it's not out of the realm of possibility that he was using this accusation as another tool to leverage the city for more money. The city council acted outraged at the mayor and his handling of the entire case. Some on the council called a press conference and vowed to have an open and transparent inquiry into the allegations against and actions of the mayor. An amazing thing took place. Once the suit was settled, Sam redirected his attention on the police and stopped making the allegations against the mayor, and the city council never mentioned gentrification again nor followed through with an open-to-the-public inquiry on the mayor's actions. Red flag #3.

I believe the mayor settled this prematurely due to a few factors. Had the lawsuit continued, witnesses would be subpoenaed and compelled to testify about the gentrification allegations. New allegations of an affair with a city employee, whom the mayor previously named as the director of Develop Louisville, had surfaced. He once posted on social media that this person had deep knowledge in land use, planning, and zoning. That sounds like the perfect witness who may have some useful insight on the claims of gentrification made by Aguiar. Witness statements would also have shown that the mayor's office did direct the Place-Based Investigations Squad to Elliott Ave. Taking the case to trial would also allow ALL the fact-based evidence to be presented to the public on a national stage. Mayor Fischer denied that Elliott Avenue was related with anything to do with his office and that he had nothing to do with directing the police to "clean up" that block. I've since been given emails that are dated months before the city put together the Place-Based Investigations Squad showing the houses that the city had already acquired and the houses that were still needed to start a new building project. Wouldn't you know, the houses targeted the night of March 13, 2020, were part of the few houses still needed to be acquired by the city. I also have the plans that were drawn up pre-2020 of the buildings they were planning on constructing on this block. The mayor can deny all he wants to about having knowledge of these plans, but his people orchestrated the emails and plans, and nothing is done in this city without the mayor's knowledge. Continuing this lawsuit would have exposed that Mayor Fischer knew the truth in the case all along and refused to set the record straight. No wonder it was settled so quickly.

The police had put a packet together to show the nexus between Breonna Taylor and Jamarcus Glover. It included transcripts from jail phone calls by Glover stating Breonna held his (dope) money and that of several others as well. It contained photos I previously referenced about the package and vehicles. This document would have played a critical part in dispelling the narrative presented by the ambulance-chasing lawyers. Representatives from the FOP had a meeting with Fischer and presented him with these documents early on in the case. Fischer pushed the documents back across his desk and said he had no use for them. Fischer was negligent to the officers under his command. He was negligent to business owners in Louisville. He was negligent in his response to the allegations which led to the protests. He was negligent to his constituents. His incompetence and negligence led to eleven people being shot during protests and one person's death. And this guy is the president of the United States Conference of Mayors. He's more suitable to be the president of the Three Ring Clown Circus. Why else would the city offer up such a penitence? The city already fired people, changed policy, and had given up an entire city block. That wasn't due to guilt or innocence. That was simply the execution of poor leadership and decision making at the top.

After they announced this unprecedented settlement, Mayor Fischer and Mike O'Connell allowed the family attorneys and Ms. Palmer, Breonna's mom, to speak. While not a normal practice, I could somewhat understand the reasoning behind this since it was such a huge case. However, the others allowed to speak had no business on that official stage, but this had been par for the course in this slanted propaganda attack.

Tamika Mallory was one of the main instigators that left Louisville in shambles. Her angry rhetoric and justice organization Until Freedom came into Louisville and continually stirred up the community. They are like the kid in class that hypes up and convinces other kids to do something they shouldn't. Then when that kid gets in trouble, they slip out the back door unscathed. They are pot-stirrers and benefit financially in huge ways. They are, for all intents and purposes, for-profit protesters, and that profit comes from propagating lies and capitalizing on the tragic deaths of people of color. In her statement Mallory said, "A settlement is restitution, but it's not arresting the cops, and we want to say today that the police officers responsible for killing Breonna Taylor must be arrested in order for the community to feel calm." Mallory continued, "We cannot forget about any of those officers, and if this police department is to do right by this community, they should be arrested and indicted immediately. Again, the restitution portion is one part, but arresting the officers is what will make this city do right by its citizens."[15]

Keturah Herron, policy strategist for the ACLU of Kentucky and member of Black Lives Matter Louisville, was also given the podium. "To Breonna Taylor's family: You deserve better than having to fight for six months after officers from Louisville Metro Police Department, some of whom remain nameless, killed your beloved family member. We are creating something different. We are creating a community that no longer invests our tax dollars in people who kill our neighbors." Herron continued, "Understand that this is not over. We are demanding for individual accountability and institutional accountability. While the culture of white supremacy has lied to you about what accountability means, let me tell you: Accountability includes self-reflection, repair, apology and changed behavior. Changed behavior means no longer incentivized violence to abuse and kill our people."[16]

The only voices allowed to speak for the previous six months were those of the group now given the stage for the announcement. Once again, they used this opportunity to demand the officers involved be arrested and charged with Breonna's death. Letter of the law be damned. Truth be damned. Once again Mayor Fischer allowed his public forum to be used to promote vengeance.

[15] Graham Ambrose, "City of Louisville to Pay Settlement to Breonna Taylor's Family," NPR, September 15, 2020, https://www.npr.org/2020/09/15/913246572/city-of-louis-ville-to-pay-settlement-to-breonna-taylors-family.

[16] Emma Austin, "What Louisville mayor, attorneys and Breonna Taylor's family said about the settlement," *Courier Journal*, September 15, 2020, https://www.courier-jour-nal.com/story/news/local/breonna-taylor/2020/09/15/breonna-taylor-settlement-what-ev-eryone-said-during-press-conference/5807508002/.

CHAPTER 11

THE DECISION

The next nine days seemed to creep by. The city was on edge, and rumors continued to fly. I can't tell you how many calls and texts my family and I received from friends trying to verify rumors they heard. Good-intentioned people, who worked in a variety of professions downtown, reached out on a daily basis with new information from their higher-ups that the decision was coming on a specific day. Most of them were wrong, but I appreciated the concern. I called people in the know at the police department, and no one knew anything, or they weren't telling me. I talked to other public safety officials who were directly involved in the planning of safety measures for the downtown area, and they were not given an exact day. The attorney general's office did an amazing job at keeping a lid on the investigation. There were no leaks, and there certainly was not collusion or a cover-up taking place as has been alleged.

My family came to our location on a couple different occasions when the rumors of a decision seemed to be imminent. I could see the angst on my mother's face, and that weighed heavy on me. My dad is an eternal optimist and continually encouraged me, but I could still see the concern. We were wrong a couple times, and everyone was becoming frustrated. We wanted this over as much as anyone else did. The mental anguish that goes with charges hanging over your head gets pretty heavy after a while. A couple of days before the decision was released, my wife said we needed to get a plan together. I asked her what she meant, even though I knew. She was referring to the possibility of me being indicted. She asked what we would tell our son, and what would she do? I assured her I was going to be okay, but all this worry had me second-guessing myself. Would the attorney general's office fold to the pressure, or would they go by the letter of the law?

I received a call from a reliable source telling me the decision was going to be released on Monday, September 21. My family gathered as we had before and anxiously waited. Some of us paced while others buried their faces in their phones trying to keep their minds occupied. The feeling in the room was different: quiet, no board games being played. The time we were told that the decision would be announced came and went and still nothing. Eventually, everyone went to bed that night with the anticipation of the decision looming over us. Most of my angst was coming from the worry I had for the police officers who were stuck dealing with a bloodthirsty mob just looking for any reason to release its anger on them. They wanted their pound of flesh in retaliation for the miscarriage of justice they had been led to believe took place. What I did next is something I have no regret doing. I would do it again if I were in the same position.

I was sitting on a couch in the basement where we were staying. My wife and son were asleep. My mind wouldn't shut off, so I decided to put my thoughts in an email to the people that were consuming those thoughts. I couldn't help but think: had things gone differently that night, then Breonna would be alive, us officers involved would still have our anonymity, and these officers that were stuck dealing with the fallout wouldn't be in harm's way. I typed out the now infamous email.

It was raw and real. I didn't polish it up and redo it. I simply typed out what I felt and sent it. I knew by this time, with all the sensitive information that had come out, that there were people on the department who were responsible for the leaks and there was a chance someone would put this out. Sam Aguiar and local anti-police reporters were getting too much inside info without there being a leak. I'm pretty sure both the FBI and I know who those leaks were, but thankfully that's not my problem now.

This email was sent only to police personnel, and it was only intended to address these individuals. I've heard and read people's slanted views and out-of-context responses to it. There was this fake disbelief and outrage that I wasn't remorseful or apologetic for what happened. That was not the purpose of this email. I was addressing the men and women who were preparing to go into the unknown territory that lay ahead. Some in

URGENT PLEASE READ!!!!

 Mattingly, Jonathan   ...
To: LMPD All Sworn
Tue 9/22/2020 2:09 AM

LMPD Family,

I'm not here to give you a Rah Rah you got this speech. I'm not here to tell you that you signed up to help this community and to keep your head up. I'm here to tell you I'm sorry you have to go through this. I'm sorry your families have to go through this. I'm sorry the Mayor, Amy Hess and Chief Conrad failed all of us in epic proportions for their own gain and to cover their asses.

You DO NOT DESERVE to be in this position. The position that allows thugs to get in your face and yell, curse and degrade you. Throw bricks, bottles and urine on you and expect you to do nothing. It goes against EVERYTHING we were all taught in the academy. The position that if you make a mistake during one of the most stressful times in your career, the department and FBI (who aren't cops and would piss their pants if they had to hold the line) go after you for civil rights violations. Your civil rights mean nothing, but the criminal has total autonomy.

We all signed up to be police officers. We knew the risks and were willing to take them, but we always assumed the city had your back. We wanted To do the right thing in the midst of an evil world to protect those who cannot protect themselves. To enforce laws that make it possible to live in a peaceful society. We as police DO NOT CARE if you are black, white, Hispanic, Asian, what you identify as...this week. We aren't better than anyone. This is not an us against society, but it is good versus evil. We are sons, daughters, husbands, wives, parters, brothers, sisters, dads and moms. We are human beings with flaws, feelings and emotions.

Now I'm just rambling, but I want you to know that I'm still proud to be a cop. To be an LMPD cop. No matter the ineptitude in upper command or the mayors office, this is one of the greatest jobs on earth. With that being said these next few days are going to be tough. They are going to be long, they are going to be frustrating. They will put a tremendous amount of stress on your families. Do not let your ego get you in a trick bag. Have your partners 6. De escalate if possible. DO NOT give the pencil pushers at the top, you know the ones who are too scared to hold the line, a reason to open investigations on you. The same ones that couldn't make decisions to save their lives. We need leaders that lead from the front and not in a room under a desk. Do what you need to do to go home you your family. Just do it with dignity and make sure you can justify your actions because everything down there is recorded.

I don't know a lot of you guys/gals but I've felt the love. Regardless of the outcome today or Wednesday, I know we did the legal, moral and ethical thing that night. It's sad how the good guys are demonized, and criminals are canonized. Put that aside for a while, keep your focus and do your jobs that you are trained and capable of doing. Don't put up with their shit, and go home to those lovely families and relationships.

I wish I were there with you leading the charge. I'll be praying for your safety. Remember you are just a pawn in the Mayors political game. I'm proof they do not care about you or your family, and you are replaceable. Stay safe and do the right thing. YOU ARE LOVED AND SUPPORTED by most of the community. Now go be the Warriors you are, but please be safe! None of these "peaceful" protesters are worth your career or freedom. God speed boys and girls.

Sgt. John Mattingly

the media assumed I had been drinking when I sent it due to the time of night and spelling of my name. Not a drop of alcohol was consumed, and I was coherent and fully aware of what I was doing. Was the email a grammatical work of art? Hardly, but thank God that's not a prerequisite for the job I do. With the insight I've given you on my opinion and issues with the upper command in the FBI, Fischer, Hess, and cowardly LMPD leadership at the time, I hope you see and feel the passion in this email now. I've had to apologize to FBI agents I know because I was not clear that I was talking about the political hacks who are just aspiring to rise in the ranks and make a name for themselves. The majority of the FBI and police are great people who are doing the job for all the right reasons, and I respect and support that. However, there are snakes in every department. That goes for the Feds, state, and local police. I've seen and experienced it at all levels over the past twenty-one years.

Let me quickly break down the email from my point of view and with my original intent in mind. First, the use of the word *thug.* You would have thought I used the N-word with the collective gasp of virtue-signaling antagonists everywhere. I received countless criticism from people for using a word that describes a person who commits the exact things I described. I never associated the word *protester* with thug, yet every single outraged person and news outlet said I called the protesters thugs. These same people said black people take offense to the word thug. If my memory serves me well, there were just as many white people committing these thuggish acts during these protests. This was another example of the media malfeasance that had taken place from day one in this case. If I, as a police officer, were to get in anyone's face and yell, curse and degrade them, throw bricks, bottles, and urine on them, I would be called a thug, as I should be. There's nothing in that statement that mentioned protesters because those are not the actions of protesting. They are, however, the actions of a thug. A thug isn't black or white. A thug isn't male or female. A thug is determined by actions and actions alone. So, get over your virtue signaling, put your big boy/girl panties on, and call a spade a spade.

Second, the meat of the email was ignored. Why we do what we do—to do the right thing, protect those who can't protect themselves, and live in a peaceful society. Who we do it for—everyone regardless of race, gender, or ethnicity. Our humanity as police officers—not police vs society, but evil vs good, and the fact we are not special but fallible human beings just like anyone else. I then exhort these men and women to do the right thing and de-escalate when possible.

The next part made people's heads explode. I said we did the legal, moral, and ethical thing that night. That was *not* referring to taking a life. Legally, we defended our lives after being fired upon. Morally, we were there that night trying to get drugs off the street that were killing people and ruining families. Ethically, we were there legally and not committing a crime as had been alluded. The very people, slimy attorneys, and media who had attacked us and accused us of heinous crimes were appalled that I would defend myself.

Last, I was criticized for telling the officers to go be the warriors they are. Liberals are screaming they don't want the police to have a warrior mentality. My question is, why not? I want the bravest and most capable warrior protecting my family and community. Had I not had a warrior mentality the night I was shot, I would've rolled over and died. You must have the proper mindset to not only survive a critical incident, but to survive a long career in this calling. The law-abiding citizens want the police to have a warrior mentality while the criminals would prefer a soft and scared police force so they can run amuck.

Wednesday, September 23, 2020: the tension in the air was so thick you could cut it with a knife. I had still heard nothing official as we did not get a heads-up that the decision was coming. The news stations broke the story that Daniel Cameron had sent out a release saying a decision would be announced at 1:30 p.m. Things just got more real than they had been in a long time. Soon I would find out my fate and the fate of my friends who were defending me that night.

When I get focused in on something, my wife says I look angry. My nose flares, my lips tighten up, and I become really quiet. My answers to questions turn into one-word responses, and my brain locks in on the moment. That is typically when she asks me repeatedly, "Are you okay?" My response is always, "I'm good." When the judge appeared on the television, the room was so quiet you could hear a pin drop. My wife and I were sitting on one couch, my two brothers-in-law on the other couch, and everyone else was standing. Judge Annie O'Connell, daughter of County Attorney Mike O'Connell, was the circuit court judge presiding over the case. That name becomes important later on. As she began to read the grand jury verdict, she read several wanton endangerment charges against Brett Hankison. O'Connell then said, "This concludes the grand jury for September 23, 2020."

My wife looked at me with tears in her eyes and said, "Is that it?" I could only nod "yes" as I had a lump in my throat. While I felt a great deal of relief that I did not hear my name attached to any charges, I could not be excited. One of my friends, one of my coworkers, and the guy who thought he was saving my life had just been indicted on some rounds that passed through the apartment walls and into another apartment. The department had already turned their back on Brett in June. The scathing letter that then acting Chief Robert Schroeder wrote was damning and placed the nail in his coffin three months before the grand jury decision. His name and reputation have been smeared all over the television for things that were untrue and not related to this case.

Daniel Cameron gave a press conference after the grand jury decision was read during which he explained in fairly good detail the reasons for not charging Myles and myself. Cameron then admonished the celebrities and Crump for their divisiveness and misinformation smear campaigns. "This is the Ben Crump model," Cameron said. "He goes into a city, creates a narrative, cherry-picks facts to establish, to prove that narrative, creates chaos in a community, misrepresents the facts, and then he leaves with his money, and then asks the community to pick up the pieces. It is terribly offensive on his part to push such narratives, such falsehoods."[17] YES! This was what I had been screaming from the mountaintop for months. This was the first person I'd heard stand up to this man. Everyone else cowered down and got out the checkbook.

Listening to him talk that day was kind of like a dream. I remember him talking but didn't hear a lot of what he was saying due to the fact my sisters and mom were crying, and my mind just kept thinking about Brett. When it was over, we all hugged, and my dad said a prayer thanking the Lord that the truth prevailed and that Daniel Cameron did not fold to the pressure like many others.

Daniel Cameron was crucified by the black community. The same group that would only be satisfied with a public square hanging of the police called him out for taking the side of the law instead of the side of black. He was called an Uncle Tom, sellout, traitor, and many an expletive. The phrase "You may be skinfolk, but you ain't kinfolk" was used. Tamika Mallory spewed, "Daniel Cameron is no different than the sellout Negroes that sold our people into slavery." Once again, the entire narrative was racially divisive and driven.

People called and texted to congratulate me, and I thanked them, but there was no real reason for me to celebrate. There was no winner in this

---

[17] Celine Castronuovo, "Kentucky attorney general takes aim at lawyer for Breonna Taylor's family: 'This is the Ben Crump model,'" *The Hill*, October 6, 2020, https://thehill.com/homenews/state-watch/519783-kentucky-attorney-general-takes-aim-at-attorney-for-breonna-taylors.

entire scenario. Attorney General Cameron potentially committed political suicide for doing the lawful thing. Breonna Taylor was still dead. Her family was still hurting. Our city had been torn apart and was in turmoil. The lives and careers of those of us involved in the incident had been torn apart, and now one of our partners was going to jail. And to top it all off, I knew my brothers and sisters in Louisville were in for a tumultuous night and days ahead. What I didn't know was that the night would end with two police officers shot.

Keep inviting the protesters to our city, Mr. Mayor. Keep allowing antagonizers to use your platform to call for our heads and stir the city into a frenzy. Once again, Mr. Mayor, your actions set this train in motion. Your inactions fueled the train. Your incompetence and ego allowed the train to run over two more cops, all while you hid in a secure, guarded location shining your virtue signal in the air like you're summoning Batman.

I continued watching the news channel to monitor the climate in Louisville, but I also switched the channel to a few of the national news stations and listened to those idiots make claims that the neighbors' walls received more justice than Breonna Taylor, that walls were more important than black lives.

Kentucky's own George Clooney was quick to weigh in the day the decision was released. In a statement given to *People*, Clooney began by addressing the Kentucky Attorney General Daniel Cameron's earlier comment that "there will be celebrities, influencers and activists who have never lived in Kentucky who try to tell us how to feel." Clooney began, "I was born and raised in Kentucky. Cut tobacco on the farms of Kentucky. Both my parents and my sister live in Kentucky. I own a home in Kentucky, and I was there last month." The Oscar winner continued, "The justice system I was raised to believe in holds people responsible for their actions. Her name was Breonna Taylor, and she was shot to death in her bed by 3 white police officers, who will not be charged with any crime for her death." Clooney concluded, "I know the community. I know the commonwealth. And I was taught in the school and churches of Kentucky what is right and what is wrong. I'm ashamed of this decision."[18]

For what it's worth, I am ashamed of the ignorance, that after six months of the facts being out, Clooney still believed Taylor was asleep in

[18] Jennifer Drysdale, "George Clooney Ashamed of Decision in Breonna Taylor Case," ET Online, September 23, 2020, https://www.etonline.com/george-clooney-ashamed-of-decision-in-breonna-taylor-case-153582.

her bed when she was tragically shot. Let me reiterate for those of you in the back of the room. We NEVER made entry into the apartment!

The internet once again blew up. Our names were trending for all the wrong reasons, and the misinformation train left the station once again. Almost immediately, the call for Daniel Cameron to release the transcripts of the grand jury proceedings began. The grand jury is set up to be private in order to protect the jurors from public scrutiny. This allows for a fair and impartial jury without the fear of retaliation.

"It's time to post all the information," Governor Andy Beshear said on MSNBC. "All the facts, all the interviews, all the evidence, all the ballistics, to truly let people look at the information. One of the problems we've had over the last six months is a total lack of explanation and information," he added. "And the vacuum that's created there—our emotions, frustrations—can truly fill that. It's time for people . . . to be able to come to their own conclusions about justice."[19] This was coming from the guy who allowed all of the misinformation, lies, and hate to be spewed from his official platform. He concluded with this gem: "Those that are currently feeling frustration, feeling hurt, they deserve to know more."[20] They deserved to know more the moment the lies began. Nothing was said about the police officers' lives that had been impacted by the government's inadequacies and shortcomings in this case. Everyone's feelings matter to these political hacks except the people who put their lives on the line every day to protect these very hacks.

Later that evening, the protests had increased in their intensity. Random gunshots could be heard on the live streamer's videos. Crowds had become unruly, and police were dispatched to the area of the gunshots. While police were attempting to clear out the large unruly crowd, more shots began to ring out. People began to scatter, and shortly after, it was discovered that two police officers had been shot. I received a text at almost the same exact time I saw the event unfold on a live streamer's Facebook video. A lump formed in my throat as the hairs on my neck stood

[19] Erik Ortiz, "Evidence in Breonna Taylor case stirs fight between Kentucky Gov. Beshear and AG Cameron," NBC News, September 24, 2020, https://www.nbcnews.com/news/us-news/evidence-breonna-taylor-case-stirs-fight-between-kentucky-gov-beshear-n1240970.

[20] https://www.nbcnews.com/news/us-news/evidence-breonna-taylor-case-stirs-fight-between-kentucky-gov-beshear-n1240970

up. My entire body felt weak once again—I felt somewhat responsible. My response to the text was, *Are they alive and who was it?*

I screen-recorded the live streamer's video and began to play it back in slow motion. You could see the moment that the suspect pointed his gun in the direction of the large group of officers and began to shoot. I sent screenshots to those I was communicating with, in case they did not know this video existed. I wanted those in charge of the investigation to have it.

I soon found the names of the officers involved. Major Aubrey Gregory had been shot in the thigh, and it appeared to not hit anything that was life-threatening. I've known Major Gregory for years and always respected him. He's one of the good ones and is a leader that isn't scared to lead from the front. The second officer I've never met, Officer Robinson Desroches. Officer Desroches's injuries were more severe. The bullet just missed his ballistic carrier and penetrated his abdomen. Several surgeries later and a few scary touch-and-go moments, he was finally released from the hospital. I talked to Desroches's supervisor in mid 2021, and he doesn't believe Desroches will be able to return to work due to his injuries. Both of their families' lives will forever be impacted by the senseless violence these two heroes endured that night. All of this could have been avoided had the right people been willing to do the right thing.

Major Aubrey Gregory   Officer Robinson Desroches

This was just the beginning of continued weeks and months of protests that the officers had to endure. During this period LMPD had mass defections due to lack of support. The younger officers have no retirement system, low pay with horrible insurance benefits, and now a city that refuses to back them even when in the right. I don't blame these guys one bit, but I hate to see Louisville lose so many great cops to other departments.

The day after the police officers were shot, Kentucky State Representative Attica Scott was arrested during the protests. A library had been set afire while a group she was with was near the incident. The police locked the group up and charged them accordingly. I don't know what probable

cause the police had, and I can't say if they were in the right or in the wrong. I do know Attica Scott was very vocal about her displeasure for the police. While the police approached the group, Ms. Scott can be heard on video saying, "Okay. Y'all, they want to kill us." No, the police don't want to kill anyone. As a matter of fact, none of the officers forced to be there that night even wanted to be there. Right, wrong, or indifferent, the "optics" of what happened next seemed a bit odd. I mentioned earlier that Circuit Court Judge Annie O'Connell is County Attorney Mike O'Connell's daughter. Attica Scott and Annie O'Connell appear to be good friends. Mike O'Connell dismissed all charges on the seventeen people arrested that night. "County Attorney O'Connell determined that this was the fair and just disposition for these individuals and for the community," the office said in a statement. "Judges dismissed charges against 17 individuals today, with one case docketed for next week on our motion to dismiss."[21]

I'm not accusing anyone of wrongdoing. I'm pointing out the hypocrisy of politicians. Optics play a major role according to those in charge . . . until it involves them.

---

[21] Taylor Weiter, "Judge drops all charges against Attica Scott, other protesters," WHAS11, November 16, 2020, https://www.whas11.com/article/news/local/attica-scott-breonna-taylor-protest-charges-dropped/417-ae2a49b6-e7c7-4037-b0dd-c11384869012.

CHAPTER 12

THE MITIGATION OF MY STORY

My attorneys have been approached by every large media outlet in the United States requesting interviews. After the attorney general's decision not to indict came down, we decided it was time to get the truth out. The city had already voluntarily paid out its largest ever lawsuit prior to the "no true bill" (a grand jury's decision that there is not probable cause to indict). That decision by the city caused many to speculate and assume we were guilty. Why else would the city give that much money before any charges were decided on if the officers involved weren't guilty? If I weren't intimately involved, I may have questioned this as well.

My attorneys talked to several national outlets and landed on ABC, thinking it would be best to do the interview in conjunction with our local paper, the *Courier Journal.* They had reached out many times asking for an interview or quotes, and they are a *Gannett*-owned paper, so the potential to reach a large audience in just one interview was appealing. I was given the choice on which anchor or personality I could go with. I chose Michael Strahan. He is a black man and always came across as someone relatable on television. Some news people are just too stuffy, and I wanted someone I felt comfortable talking to.

Due to COVID-19 restrictions, we couldn't go to New York to do the interview, and if they came to Kentucky, they'd have to quarantine upon return. They decided on a location in Cincinnati. The night before the interview, we went to dinner with my attorneys and the producers of *Good Morning America* and *20/20.* We talked to the producers while we ate a good meal so they could get a better feel for us and how they wanted to approach the interview. The night went well, and we walked back to our hotel with high hopes for the interview the next day.

The following morning we drove to the location and were asked to wait in a trailer until they had Strahan ready to go. I was a little nervous. I had never been in front of the cameras and wasn't sure how these types of things went. I didn't know if I'd make a fool of myself or if the media crew were going to be jerks (they weren't, by the way). When they brought us into the room where we'd be filming, I could see them placing the microphone on Strahan's lapel. They ushered me to the stool where I would spend the next three hours defending myself. They adjusted the lights and did a few quick screen tests. Strahan walked up, and we acknowledged one another. He sat down, and the interview began. There was no warm-up time and no small talk. The clapperboard sounded, and off we went.

Right out of the gate, Strahan attempted to put me on my heels. I had seen the interviews done with Kenneth Walker and saw the coddling he received from his interviewees. They allowed him to express himself, and it was as if they could feel his pain—even though each of his interviews had a different tale to tell. That wasn't the case on this interview. Every question was as much an accusation or assumption as it was a question. It was like three hours on the witness stand being cross-examined by a defense attorney. Strahan's mind was made up before the interview, and his facial expressions and body language showed that. The rapport was good, but there was never a time he was able to see things from my perspective. When my answer wasn't to his liking, he'd follow it up with another question, trying to trip me up.

I spoke the truth and didn't mince my words. Professional interviewers and politicians tend to give the runaround and deflect. I wanted the truth out. I wanted people to see what had been done to those of us involved due to the media misinformation machine. Strahan was visibly upset or disagreed with some of my answers. There were a couple times it became chippy, but it was never disrespectful.

When the interview ended, we talked for a few minutes. Strahan was cordial and professional. I'm a Dallas Cowboys fan and have been since I could remember watching football. Strahan asked me why a guy in Kentucky was a Cowboys fan. I told him it was because my dad was, and that's all I knew. He then said, "I like you other than the fact you are a Cowboys fan." We wrapped up that portion of the interview and had a break for lunch. Strahan left, and it was now time for the *Courier Journal*'s shot at me.

The *Courier* has dedicated a lot of resources and time to this story. Some stories felt biased against us, while others seemed like actual neutral journalism. The reporters were kind and seemed more open minded and compassionate than Strahan. Some reporters at the *Courier* are very open about their anti-police agenda, and some remain neutral. I try my best not to cast a net over an entire organization because I hate it when one cop does something wrong and we all get that tag placed on us. Nonetheless, I was skeptical about giving the *Courier* any access to me, but I must admit these journalists gave me a fair shake on this interview.

I was mentally exhausted after the interviews. Hours of questions and defending yourself in a strange environment will wear you down. Then, we anxiously awaited the release of the story to see what angle was taken.

The story was originally released on ABC's *Good Morning America*. Strahan sat on stage with Robin Roberts and George Stephanopoulos. The attitude was dismissive and one of shock and awe at some of my answers. I get it. Strahan couldn't say anything positive about me or he would run the risk of being canceled. Or maybe he really disliked me and is just a good actor. What I said was twisted and not in full context. I knew this was the probability when we did the interview, but I thought it was worth the chance. What did I have to lose at this point? Character assassination had already taken place for months. ABC cut out all the positive points that were made and chose to edit the shows in a light in which I appeared cocky or tone deaf to the issues between police and the black community. When you hold the power of edit in your control, you can make anything seem as you want it to appear. They used a total of about five minutes of interviews out of the three hours recorded. Again, that's okay. I've come to accept the mainstream media will not report the truth if there's a chance it will disprove the narrative that they've invested so much energy into.

Naturally, the story was all about Breonna and Kenny being victimized. Again, I'm okay with lifting up Breonna's name. She was sincerely an unintentional victim in this case. I do feel for her family. She did not deserve to die. But that's not the entire story. The media will fail the truth every time. The story presented on *GMA* and *20/20* was nothing short of a hit piece. The interviews were slanted, which was expected, but I had hoped for them to push Kenneth Walker like they did me. He was coddled and allowed to change his story once again without any follow-up questions.

Regardless, I was able to tell MY truth. I was able to air it out to a room full of people who heard the unedited, real truth. That was satisfying to me. Strahan can get on TV and shake his head at a twisted clip, but if he has any intuition—and he's a bright man—he could tell I'm not this racist monster I've been portrayed as.

The real kicker was an op-ed in the *Courier Journal* by one of their writers, Joseph Gerth. The *Courier* begged to be a part of this story. When I finally and begrudgingly agreed to let them in with ABC, they seemed appreciative. However, once the story was released by Gerth's own newspaper that had asked to interview me, here's what this pompous jerk had to say:

**Louisville officer at center of Breonna Taylor case
needs to just stop talking**
JOSEPH GERTH
Louisville Courier Journal

Someone needs to take Louisville Metro Police Sgt. Jonathan Mattingly aside, and tell him to be quiet.

The couple of times he's opened his mouth or sent out a group email, he's reminded us what is wrong with policing in Louisville.

It happened when he sent out an email last month that characterized those protesting the shooting death of Breonna Taylor as "thugs." [**LIE #1** I never mentioned protesters and thugs together.]

And it happened again in an interview with The Courier Journal and ABC News on Tuesday, when he appeared to suggest George Floyd died from a drug overdose and, if he didn't, he got what was coming to him because he was "not a model citizen." [**LIE #2** that was never said in any form or fashion. Maybe Joe should be a fiction writer.]

Talk about tone deaf.

Mattingly was the first police officer to rush into Taylor's apartment March 13. He took a slug to his thigh when Taylor's boyfriend, Kenneth Walker, fired at him. He responded by squeezing off several rounds in Walker's direction.

It was the first interview Mattingly has given since a Jefferson County grand jury didn't indict him after Attorney General Daniel Cameron ruled he fired in self-defense.

In the same interview Tuesday, Mattingly also said in his view, good police don't use racial profiling but do use "criminal profiling."

Mattingly explained "criminal profiling" is looking for people who don't make eye contact with police, go the other direction when they see an officer or do the sorts of things any of us would do if we had learned from a young age that police are a danger to us.

The same sorts of things we would all do if we were Black and had lived long enough to recall the deaths of Botham Jean, Philando Castile, Eric Garner, Trayvon Martin, Tamir Rice, Michael Brown and so many others.

The same sorts of things we would all do if we were Black and were once given "the talk" by a father or uncle or mother about how to get home alive if we had a run in with a police officer.

When I was a child, I was taught if you were in trouble and needed help, you looked for a police officer.

Young Black children are often taught the opposite now. Avoid the police at all costs.

For whatever reason, police officers and many of those they are charged to protect take on an "us" versus "them" attitude.

It's understandable why police might get that attitude, especially if they work in neighborhoods where guns and drugs are everywhere, and the homicide rate is soaring. It's a dangerous job.

They are fearful. They want to get home to their families each night.

I get it.

But the problem is the vast majority of people in the community—the people they police—aren't the drug dealers or gangbangers.

They're just people struggling to get by every day and pay the bills.

They're folks whose worst crime may be speeding or perhaps smoking a joint every now and again or walking home drunk after a night with some buddies.

Let's be clear. Refusing to make eye contact with a police officer is not a crime. Nor is turning the other direction when one pulls up beside you when you're driving.

It might be someone chooses not to make eye contact because they had something else on their mind.

Or they had rolled through a stop sign a couple of streets back and didn't want to do anything more that might draw an officer's attention.

And marching downtown to protest police brutality doesn't make someone a "thug."

They might be just someone who has seen too many grieving parents after cases like Taylor's.

Or they might be pretty ticked off at cops—all cops—because the last time they were there protesting, police fired pepper balls at them or filled their lungs with tear gas.

In the interview, Mattingly said he was only referring those protesters who did things like spit on police, throw Molotov cocktails and destroy property when he used the word "thugs."

"You DO NOT DESERVE to be in this position," he wrote in the email. "The position that allows thugs to get in your face and yell, curse and degrade you. Throw bricks bottles and urine on you and expect you to do nothing."

We've got a problem in Louisville with police and how they get along with the people they are supposed to protect. We've got a problem with how some of those same people react to police.

But the thing is, we're not going to get beyond this as long as we have police officers who are willing to discount the death of someone like Floyd because he wasn't a model citizen. [LIE #3 I said on national TV it was HORRIBLE and I thought that officer would go to prison.]

We're also not going to get beyond this as long as police view people as criminals simply because they don't make eye contact or veer away when they see a police officer coming their direction. [LIE #4 That was not the context of the story and he knows it. I said those were some of the psychological indicators that someone is trying to avoid the police. I also said it's not one of these things, but a combination.]

We're not going to get beyond it as long as police view those who question their actions as nothing more than "thugs."

Joseph Gerth can be reached at 502-582-4702 or by email at jgerth@ courierjournal.com. Support strong local journalism by subscribing today.[22]

Joseph Gerth, I'll shut my mouth when you actually start reporting facts and not emotion, but I don't see that happening any time soon.

---

[22] October 21, 2020, https://www.courier-journal.com/story/opinion/columnists/ gerth/2020/10/21/jonathan-mattingly-makes-police-look-worse-each-thing-he- says/3717828001/

That is the only interview we have conducted to this point. It didn't get presented as well as we'd hoped by ABC, but that was expected due to the sad state of America right now.

While getting my story out about the events that preceded March 13 and the actual event are important, it's equally important to express my disbelief in the missteps the city made along the way. If the story of Ms. Palmer is accurate, then she was not treated appropriately at the scene or by the department following the death of her daughter. I'm not disparaging the officers on scene because I wasn't there, but if it were my child and I was given the runaround, I'd be highly upset at that as well. Apparently, there was a lack of communication from the department to Ms. Palmer. I understand that frustration because I received the same treatment. I had no idea what was going on during the months that followed the incident.

Then there was the misinformation that wasn't addressed by the police department or the city. I've been very outspoken on that, and will continue to beat that drum, because I do not want this to happen to the next person in my position. And whoever thought it was a good idea to release the incident report mostly blank should have their competency checked.

On June 10, 2020 investigators traveled to the Attorney General's Office in Frankfort, Kentucky to request Digital Forensic Examiner, Mike Littrell to conduct additional examinations on the cell phones belonging to Breonna Taylor. Investigators previously obtained legal authority to forensically exam the phones. Due to a security passcode on the phone only an abbreviated examination was obtained. Mr. Littrell took custody of the cell phones pending further analysis. On June 10, 2020 LMPD Legal Advisor, Dennis Sims, made several requests for the file content to satisfy requests made through open records and the Civil Division of the Jefferson County Attorney's Office. After consulting with Deputy A.G. Amy Burke, the request was denied due to the potential prosecution of law enforcement. Investigators learned later the same day the iLeads report associated with the incident had been released by PIU Lieutenant Theodore Eidem prior to its completion. The report reflected incorrect information generated from CAD information.
It should be noted the information was publicly released without knowledge or approval of the lead investigators and prior to review for completion and accuracy The report was disseminated through multiple media sources creating a disparaging narrative towards LMPD.

I understand on sensitive cases (child molestings, rape, murder, etc.) that all the information isn't placed in the standard reports due to securing that sensitive information. Generally, the standard incident report is used to draw a case number, and the narrative will say "Refer to PIU case #_ for details." However, this was not explained when the report was released. I must admit, it looked bad. Therefore, the attorneys said it was another attempt to cover up, and the media ran with it. Furthermore, the lead investigators were not aware that the incident report was going to be released. There was a lack of communication due to downtown wanting to control the narrative.

Division: 3 DISTRICT	Incident/Investigation Report	**UNAPPROVED**
Beat: 322		
Agency: LMPD	Case Number: 80-20-017049	Case Status: OPEN ACTIVE

Supplement Information		
Supplement Date	Supplement Type	Supplement Officer
06/11/2020 17:25:48		(7599) VANCE, JASON S
Contact Name		Supervising Officer

Supplement Notes

PUBLIC NARRATIVE

Shell report containing CAD generated information which was publicly released without knowledge or approval of the lead investigator and prior to review for completion and accuracy. The report was unlocked by LMPD Records supervisor and was completed by the lead investigator.

INVESTIGATIVE NARRATIVE

Every article states somewhere in it that no drugs or money were found. This was also a mistake made by the department. When an officer is shot, our Public Integrity Unit takes over a scene, and they draw up their own search warrant so they can collect the evidence as it relates to the officer-involved shooting. They collect casings, blood samples, take photos and measurements, and collect anything related to their specific investigation. These detectives aren't there looking for narcotics and money. They are processing a scene for their investigation into the police-shooting. Period.

So once I was shot, the detectives who did the initial investigation on Glover and who were the leads on the case had to wait until PIU was finished with their warrant on the apartment and then request permission to go and execute the search warrant looking for narcotics evidence for their case. They wanted to finish the job, or everything was all in vain. However, the call came from above them that they were not allowed to search. *To this day I do not know why that decision was made.* There may have been no ill will intended when the decision was made, but it shed a cloud of doubt over the case that can't be removed. We know for a fact from the jail phone calls that two different people retrieved money from that apartment after the police left. Were there drugs hidden by Walker or Taylor that weren't discussed on the calls? We will never know. It was a fatal mistake that guided the narrative of the case going forward. It haunts me to this day.

A huge point of contention was the fact that there was no body camera footage of this tragedy. When I transferred to Narcotics in 2016, no one in Narcotics had a body camera. The idea behind no cameras in Narcotics was the sensitive nature of the work. There are a few dynamics behind this reasoning. First, it was to avoid our tactics being easily available to the defense attorneys and bad guys. When serving warrants, you need the element of surprise. Having all our tactics available would compromise that. We also drove unmarked cars and didn't want them easily discovered because on most days we would spend hours in these unmarked cars in sketchy neighborhoods trying to blend in while conducting surveillance. If the target of the investigation knows all our vehicles, then that puts the detectives in danger and the operation is a bust. The main reasoning for no body cameras was the use of informants and keeping their identities anonymous. When a drug suspect decides to flip and become a snitch, it's a very dangerous path for them and they know it. Their safety becomes the responsibility of their handler (i.e., the narcotics detective). Having a camera perched up on your shoulder would deter many people from turning on these dangerous drug dealers. Defense attorneys would catch on rather quickly and use open records to dime out the informants to their clients. I know it's hard to believe that a defense attorney would cross that ethical line, but some do. I'm not bashing defense attorneys because there are many upstanding attorneys, but we all know the ones I'm talking about.

During my career I was always against body cameras, not because I was doing anything shady or illegal, but who likes Big Brother watching your every move? My stance on that has changed! *I so wish we, or at least I, had a body camera on that night.* I would love for the world to see the truth and not just hear it. It's a sad day when the criminal element is believed ahead of seven officers with over 120 years combined of street experience. I'd beg for a body camera if I were ever to go back to policing. Body cameras have been proven to clear officers against false claims in the vast majority of cases.

In May 2020, once I was healed up enough to get out, I stopped by our work office to see a few of the guys. I ran into a detective who had an informant into the circle that Kenneth Walker ran in. He said that this source told him that as soon as Kenneth Walker got out of jail, he was allegedly back in the drug game. He had my attention, so I asked what he planned to do with that info. He sheepishly told me that they were given a stand-down order from the chief's office. They were told not to investigate Walker or anyone associated with the incident. Little did I know that optics are already playing a role in this situation. Just recently I was informed by someone close to the Public Integrity Unit investigation that once they revealed the contents of Kenneth Walker's phone to those downtown, they were also given the stand-down order. They were instructed to no longer investigate any of the allegations involving drug trafficking and home invasions that were tied to Kenneth's text messages and photos discovered during the search warrant on Walker's phone.

So, once again I would love for the mayor's office, Amy Hess, and the former head of the police department to explain the logic behind the stand-down orders to me and the public and clarify why two separate cases of potential wrongdoing by Walker weren't pursued. This is a guy who shot a police officer, has changed his story on several occasions, is suing the city in both state and federal court, has received hundreds of thousands of dollars, and is allegedly back to his old games.

I believe Walker and his attorneys saw that the city was handing out money like the federal government is stimulus checks and thought he would get in on the action while the getting was good. I'd had enough of the one-sided war against myself and the others involved. Kenneth Walker shot me and is now suing me for his mental anguish. I decided to countersue. If the city and department weren't willing to stand up and fight for what's right, I would. I almost had to laugh at all the dramatic responses from television and social media personalities. How dare the guy who was shot and almost taken from his family defend himself yet again from an attack by Kenneth Walker? While I do not look for a fight, I'm also not one to stand and take a beating. Those of us involved have been kicked over and over again while we are down. Enough already. This lawsuit isn't about money because Walker has probably blown through his 330k. This is all about principle.

A notable point of interest that arose surrounding the lawsuits that Kenneth Walker filed involved Commonwealth Attorney Tom Wine. Steven

On June 11, 2020 Investigators were ordered to stop all proactive investigative actions by close of business on June 12, 2020. Investigators along with LMPD CSU personnel traveled outside of Jefferson County to an undisclosed location to obtain a DNA standard for Sergeant Jon Mattingly. Sergeant Mattingly provided written consent to obtain the standard in the form of a buccal swab. Investigators returned to the PIU office working through the night to complete the outstanding investigative tasks deemed important to the investigation.

†On June 12, 2020 investigators had an unscheduled meeting with Interim Police Chief Robert Schroeder and Louisville Metro Chief of Public Services Amy Hess. Chief Hess was provided a briefing on the case and was informed of the outstanding investigative actions needed to be fulfilled by investigators.

Investigators requested to seek legal authority to obtain Kenneth Walker's DNA standard and were denied the request by Louisville Metro Chief of Public Services Amy Hess. Investigators were informed prior approval would be needed before taking any further police action in the investigation.

Romines, attorney for Kenneth Walker, stated on a podcast with Professor Ricky Jones of the University of Louisville that he told Tom Wine he would drop him from the lawsuit if he would permanently dismiss the charges on Kenneth Walker. This would mean the charges for shooting me could not be revisited if more evidence arose (i.e., the call to Kenneth Walker's mother stating the police were at the door). The day before the deadline for the lawsuit, March 8, 2021, Tom Wine announced that the charges would be dropped with prejudice. I now had no legal recourse against my assailant. The slap in the face is that no one from the Commonwealth's Attorney's Office or the police department reached out and let me know this. I found out through social media.

I've often speculated that, had I not been shot, I would have been fired like the others. Who would ever have thought that being shot was the best thing to happen to me that night?

CHAPTER 13

STANDING IN THE GAP

I'm often asked what I think the problem is between law enforcement and the community. My general answer is the judicial system as a whole. Repeat offenders who should still be in jail or prison are one of the biggest issues today. That may seem to be a cop-out to many, but it's the truth. If the judicial system worked like it should, we wouldn't have most of the problems we have today. Jamarcus Glover should never have been out of jail for warrants to be served that night. In January of 2020, he was locked up for drugs and weapons which is just 1 of several pending cases. In 2015 he was found guilty on drug and weapon charges. This was a pattern, and the courts missed it. Even though he had several open felony cases, the courts continued to make him promise he would be a good boy and they'd let him out. He promised, they let him out, and he repeated the offense over and over and over. [23]This lack of accountability put several lives at risk each time he was arrested, each time warrants were served on his locations, not to mention how many lives were lost to the overdoses related to the drugs that were pushed. The uproar should be with the system and the number of repeat offenders that are let out prematurely when they commit more crimes.

One more recent example. In May 2020 an LMPD officer stopped a vehicle. The young man was out of the car talking to the officer and started to become very antsy. The officer asked the young man to not reach back in his vehicle. The individual ignored the officer's command, leaned in his car, and came back out with a pistol and shot the officer in the shoulder. The suspect was chased down by other officers. The

---

[23] https://www.wave3.com/2020/08/26/warrants-issued-arrest-breonna-taylors-ex-boy-friend-amid-leaked-new-documents/

suspect was shot, but it was not fatal. He recovered from his injuries, and the judge thought it was a good idea to place him on home incarceration. This time it was caught on body camera and is clear as day that he was intent on killing a cop that night to get away, and he got home incarceration. These judges have lost their minds. Had this been a judge shot on camera, I'm guessing they wouldn't be so lenient.

WDRB.com

Man on house arrest surrenders after standoff in Jeffersontown

Apr 11, 2021 Updated 6 hrs ago

Decedric Binford mugshot. (Photo courtesy of Louisville Metro Corrections)

LOUISVILLE, Ky. (WDRB) -- A standoff in Jeffersontown that lasted for several hours ended peacefully after the suspect surrendered Sunday evening.

Decedric Binford was charged with second-degree assault-domestic violence. He was on home incarceration for attempted murder of a police officer after he allegedly opened fire on an LMPD officer in May 2020. Former LMPD

Fast-forward to April 11, 2021. This same individual assaulted his girlfriend with a knife. Fortunately, she and her child escaped and were able to call the police. After a two-hour standoff with SWAT, he surrendered. Again, there would be no secondary victims if the offenders were held accountable by the courts for their crimes.

When I first joined the police department, I was told that this job would change me. I, like most others, said *"Not me."* I was wrong. No matter what end of town you were raised in or what you've been exposed to, you can never understand the things that police officers and first responders see. Just when you think you've seen it all, there's a new revelation waiting for you. As a result, just as citizens easily become jaded toward the police and have a one-sided view, the police become jaded as well and have a one-sided view of society. It's unhealthy for both parties.

The fact that most people only interact with the police on the worst days doesn't always lead to the opportunity to leave a positive impact on people's lives, but there are some positive stories. I have had a few occasions where I've been out and someone approached to thank me for saving their lives because of an arrest, or in some cases, because I cut them a break and allowed them the opportunity to correct the path they were going down. Those examples, unfortunately, are the exception to the rule. I wish this were Mayberry and every interaction could turn into a positive outcome, but once again this isn't television. This is a dirty business at times, and we get a look inside a society that most people will never experience.

Part of the unhealthiness is because so much is expected out of our police. We are law enforcers, psychiatrists, social workers, teachers, medical responders, marriage counselors, and the list goes on. This is the only profession that is used like a Swiss Army knife but are expected to perform with the precision of a scalpel. One mistake, or perceived mistake, and you are condemned. We must take the blame for when we screw up and must own it, but we must be supported when we do the right things as well. I've been called to houses because little Johnny wouldn't get up to go to school. That is not a police issue, but I had to respond, and now I was the bad guy no matter what the outcome was. Mom or Johnny was gonna be mad. I've made runs where a tenant won't pay a landlord. My dad owned rental properties, and most renters were a pain to deal with, but that's a civil matter and not a police matter. I can't go into a tenant's pocket and take his money to pay the landlord. Once again, I leave a bad taste in someone's mouth because we didn't do enough. When I hear police reform activists say they want to take some of the responsibilities that police have and distribute them out, I agree. (I would throw caution to domestic calls. Those are one of the most unpredictable and volatile calls to make. A social worker may help after the fact, but just sending social workers is a ticking time bomb.) Police nationwide would love to simply enforce laws and protect their community. We hate being a jack-of-all-trades as well.

Dealing with people with mental illness brings on a whole new challenge. There are officers with zero discernment. These officers give departments and the profession a bad name. If you hate your job, find a new one. If you are scared to do your job, find a new one. This job isn't for everyone. These cops will have the mentality of, *I am the police, and you must do as I say*. That rarely has a positive outcome and especially doesn't work in situations where there's someone mentally challenged or dealing with mental illness. Our department placed a big emphasis on crisis intervention several years back. While there's no perfect way to deal with all scenarios, I believe it helped the officers who deal with it on a daily basis.

One of the buzz words you hear now in policing is de-escalation. I had to give a Professional Standards Unit interview for them to judge whether I was able to de-escalate the situation of returning fire after I was shot. The funny thing about this "new" term is that de-escalation has been around for years. When I was a young officer, they used to call it verbal judo. I'm sure before it was called that, it was called something else. Probably something like "just treat people right and talk to them with some respect." I've said this for years, and I stand by it: there needs to be more training in our academies and then in our yearly re-certifications on how to talk to people.

There are some cops who are real jerks, guys I don't like because of their attitude or the way they talk to people. They are brash and insensitive. There's a time to take a hard line, but kindness achieves goals better than force in most situations.

It's very easy to become jaded in this job and to perceive an us-against-them mentality. When you are disrespected daily, it's sometimes hard to set that positive tone upon first interaction. Obviously, as police officers we help anyone and everyone in need. The guy who's cursing you, threatening you, and spitting in your face one day is often the victim you are now risking your life to save the next. There have been occasions where a person that hated me one day, for the simple fact that I was a police officer, was begging for my help the next. I never rejected that call for help, and often times I tried to use the situation as a tool to bridge the gap. The fact has never once entered my head that the person I am helping hated me and therefore I should not help them. The God-given instinct of being a protector always kicks in, and you put your human nature aside to not only help that person in need, but as I did on several occasions, I put my life in danger to help that person.

People today are quick to paint with a wide brush that all police officers are racist or power-hungry, and one would be a fool to think that either of those do not exist. However, I believe with all my heart and soul that today's police officer is the least corrupt that it's ever been in the history of our country. The people who want to demonize the police are quick to point out a few viral videos they see each year, which isn't even a drop in the bucket for the millions of interactions police have with the communities we serve. Sometimes we get it wrong. Sometimes officers need to lose their jobs or go to prison, but that's not a common ordeal.

Some people are lazy and assert the fact that police forces were created to round up slaves that escaped the treacherous and evil conditions that this country allowed to be part of its history. The 13th Amendment of the Constitution, which abolished slavery, was adopted on December 18, 1865. This country continued to see imbedded racism through most of the twentieth century. That part of American history is ungodly and unforgivable. And even though some never experienced it, they are angry over it. This anger is like a cancer to our society. One would be a fool to think racism and discrimination doesn't still exist in America. We've all seen it at some point in our lives. However, through my forty-eight years,

I have seen a significant decrease of the overt racism that I saw or heard about growing up. There are still pockets in society that have refused to evolve and to see the good in all people. I thank God that the majority of Americans don't live by those immoral standards of the past, but we must continue to educate and improve. I'm thankful that the cycle of slavery was broken and that is the history of our country and not the present. There continues to be bias and hate, but we will never rid the world of that. It's been on earth since the beginning of time and is not unique to America. We must choose love over hate, be willing to forgive, and choose to help rather than hinder.

Over the past couple of years, I have really struggled with and been heartbroken when we conduct warrants where the children are home. I've thought to myself that we are affecting these kids for the rest of their lives. Having a warrant conducted on your home is a traumatic event. While we didn't cause the parent to be a criminal, my empathy for the kids became a struggle. I did my best to coordinate times when the kids wouldn't be home, or even better, get the target of the warrant away from the house and walk them back using their key for entry. I've always been able to calm most kids down, having four of my own, and thus I would often be the one to try and preoccupy them. I'd make crazy faces trying to get them to laugh, let them play on my phone, and on a few occasions, I took pictures with them and let them see them. I did anything I could to ease their anxiety and not set a tone of total hate for the police. This is the human side of policing. When a police officer loses their empathy, it's time for a break or a career change. This job can be a thief of the heart.

Policing sometimes feels like a no-win situation. You want to enforce the laws and make the world a safer place for your kids and grandkids, but you become enemy #1 for trying to achieve that. I realize the majority of Americans either support the police or understand the necessity for law and order. I also realize from an American citizen standpoint, toeing the line of enforcing laws and government overreach is a tightrope at times. I also realize that the police cross that line at times. With cameras everywhere now, we've all seen the viral videos of a cop overstepping his/her authority. It's not a pretty picture when that takes place, and it jeopardizes the reputation of the force as a whole. I realize police are and should be held to a higher standard. We are given the ability to take a person's freedom away. That freedom is the most cherished thing about this great country and the premise on which it was founded. I also try and remind people that police are just human beings. We are fallible. We do make mistakes. Those mistakes sometimes have irreversible consequences. There is not one profession in the world where people don't make mistakes because we are all flawed human beings.

With our mistakes we must be willing to learn and grow. In my interview with the media, I stressed that I believe all Americans want the same things. We want freedom. We want to feel safe and secure. We want to be left alone by the government. We want to all be playing on an equal playing field. And I think most people want to get along with others. The big question is, how can we apply this thinking to involve the public and law enforcement?

I don't think law enforcement alone must make the effort. We all have our biases based on the way we were raised and what we were exposed to, but what helps us break those barriers is the bigger question. I don't think there's a magic wand, but I do think that, if we could point to the things we have in common as opposed to what we don't, we could make huge strides. It's a tall task. The mistrust is real. I think it's misguided in some areas, but it's real.

When I was talking to Strahan, we got into a debate over feelings. He stated that black people feel targeted by the police. The statistics do not support that, and I explained that just because you feel something doesn't make it real. A therapist may say it's your reality if you feel it, but that doesn't make it the truth. My theory about the FBI murder-for-hire investigation may not be true, but it feels that way to me. I have no hard evidence, but my gut tells me it's true. None of that makes it a reality until it is actually proven to be real. My feelings don't matter if the facts don't back them up.

Society today has made everyone feel like a victim. It's an easy trap to fall into, because people feel sorry for the victim. This entire book I've told you I was a victim, so you probably think I'm contradicting myself. The difference is in the facts. I was in fact shot. I did have to sell my house and go in hiding. I did have confirmed threats on my life. I was painted in an awful light by many. The caveat is I don't want your sympathy. I want my story to make a difference. I want society to stop insisting on someone to blame for every crisis and tragedy. I don't want another Breonna Taylor or another John Mattingly. I know there will continue to be both, as I've read stories of several officers killed this week. There were no riots. There was no mass destruction of property. There was heartache though. That's a common emotion we all feel. That's a common ground where we must come together and understand we are all humans who experience loss.

Policing is changing. With change comes growing pains. I'm all for change where it's needed, but not just for the sake of change. I believe churches should play a major role in police and citizen interaction. Churches have turned their congregations against police in some instances this past year. We need the church to be a foundation for morals and principles, not social justice platforms to attract new followers. Teach Christ's words to love your neighbor as yourself. If we would all take on the Golden Rule, we could coexist with less strife. The police are not the moral compass of society. That starts at the home and is reinforced through church. Our schools should not be the ones indoctrinating our children. Schools should exist to teach children how to think and learn. We need America to come together, or we will collapse from within. The more we hate and divide, the weaker and more vulnerable we become.

There's a gap in our country that seems to grow daily. I fear for my children and grandchildren that the divide will eventually mean an America we will not recognize. Patrick Henry was on to something when he said, "United we stand, divided we fall." We as humans can do what we can to fill the gap, but unless everyone is on the same page, that goal will never be achieved. Furthermore, we as humans will never achieve that goal on our own. God knew this, and He stood in the gap for us by sending His Son, Jesus, in human form to live as a man, die for our sins, and rise from the dead so we could be restored into a personal relationship with Him.

Ezekiel 22:30 (KJV) says, "And I sought for a man among them, that should make up the hedge, and stand in the gap before me for the land, that I should not destroy it: but I found none." Part of our responsibility as followers of Christ is to pray for God's intervention in the lives of others. God wants us to reflect His Glory by standing in that gap for others. I am praying for our country and am willing to stand in that gap for everyone. I pray that you will be willing to do this as well, and just maybe God will save our land.

There are many people well deserving of the dedication of this book. My wife, parents, children, siblings, and friends have all been rock solid. However, while I was in the midst of writing this book, I was reminded very personally of the reason I was willing to sacrifice my life for my community and fight against the poison that is spread.

My beautiful cousin, Jenna, was hanging out with some friends in a park late one evening and playing music through her car radio. As the group gathered their belongings to go home, Jenna realized the battery on her car had run down. Her friends called for a ride, but Jenna didn't want to leave her car stranded in the park. She persuaded her friends she would be fine, as she had called an acquaintance to come get her and her car. The friends were skeptical since they didn't know the guy coming to get her, but she assured them she was fine.

The next morning this beautiful, fun loving soul was found in an alley, discarded like trash. Jenna drank occasionally but never took drugs. Her autopsy found that she had ingested fentanyl through her mouth. It is believed she was given a fake pill for pain, not knowing it was a counterfeit pill pressed with deadly fentanyl.

Throughout my career I have met many grieving parents and families who have suffered the same fate. Those encounters always gave me a new resolve to try and help other families avoid this devastation. I dedicate this book to Jenna and the countless others who have lost their lives to this poison.

Jenna, we will miss your humor and quick wit. We will miss your smile and big heart. I'm sorry I couldn't do more to save you from this epidemic that takes so many lives too soon. We love you and will see you one day in Heaven.